What People Are Saying:

The Wilde Woman's Guide to Organizing in Five Simple Steps is a radical book. Joyce gets to the root of disorganization and offers questions and suggestions that will change your habits. This straightforward, easy-to-read book is both grounding and extremely liberating.

> ~ **Karen Bernard**
> **Book Buyer, East End Food Co-op, Pittsburgh, PA**

Joyce's approach in linking mindfulness with organizing is very practical, positive, and extremely helpful. I enjoy her insights and conversational style. *The Wilde Woman's Guide to Organizing in Five Simple Steps: Using Mindfulness to Change Your Habits* also aligns with my personal commitment to being mindful and living in harmony. It's a pleasure to read.

> ~ **Krishna Pendyala**
> **Author, *Beyond the PIG and the APE:***
> ***Realizing SUCCESS and true HAPPINESS***
> **and Founder of ChoiceLadder**

As a professional coach, I support people to awaken to their true selves and apply their gifts effectively to their lives and businesses. Coaching helps people change and grow. It's very difficult to create something new in your life if your life is disorganized. For that reason, I appreciate the book Joyce has written. Her focus is on changing lifestyle habits, which helps people gain full mastery of their lives. This is a perspective that deeply resonates with me.

> ~ **Suzanne Ferguson and Associates**
> **Spiritual Mastery Coaching**

My husband and his family have been in the restaurant business for over 35 years. As a result, I know that for a small business to survive and thrive, being organized is vital. Joyce is a highly skilled professional who brings a unique perspective to the organizing process. She draws not only from her Master's Degree in Psychology, but also from her valuable experience of having co-owned her own business, a restaurant. Add to this her love of communication, and empathy for those she's helping, and you've got an powerful recipe for effectiveness."

~ Wendy Cibula
Owner, Franklin Inn Mexican Restaurant

If you are in a quandary as to how to organize anything in life, including your home, office, boat or personal life, you will find Joyce Wilde's book, *The Wilde Woman's Guide to Organizing in Five Simple Steps* of great benefit. I have experienced first-hand Joyce's personal skills in helping me organize my work space, and it has already saved me countless hours of going through files to find information, and increased my energy and motivational level. Thank you, Joyce for sharing your creative and intuitive understanding of simplifying and getting rid of the clutter in our lives!

~ Glenn Freund
Physical Therapist

As a marketing enthusiast, author and creator of the Network PRo Toolkit, I really appreciate *The Wilde Woman's Guide to Organizing in Five Simple Steps* because one of the biggest challenges business owners face is how to get and stay organized for improved productivity. Networking can be overwhelming, and to be successful it is critical to have strong organizational skills. Joyce's process will empower business professionals to achieve success by providing an easy-to-use process helping them to increase networking efficiency and business growth.

~ Sheryl Johnson
Founder, BD-PRo Marketing Solutions

As a business owner, I know how important it is to be organized. I also know that good habits are vital, because in my office we do Integrated Medicine, Chiropractic, Fitness and Nutritional Analysis. A challenge my patients typically face is developing and maintaining lifestyle habits that support their health. For this reason, I appreciate *The Wilde Woman's Guide to Organizing in Five Simple Steps* because of Joyce's focus on habit formation rather than simply on "getting organized."

~ Nancy Alexandria Guzy-Venick, D.C., PA-C, RT.R
Spinal Rehab and Wellness Clinic

As a freelance writer, I know how important it is to be organized. I also know how valuable effective communication is in both my personal and work relationships. Those skills are essential to function effectively. For these reasons I appreciate Joyce Wilde's perspective in *The Wilde Woman's Guide to Organizing in Five Simple Steps*. It's entertaining, engaging and full of practical ideas for "go-with-the flow" creative people.

~ Mary Cvetan
Cvetan Communications

The Wilde Woman's Guide to Organizing
in Five Simple Steps:
Using Mindfulness to Change Your Habits

by Joyce B. Wilde, M.S.

For permission, please contact joyce@joycewilde.com. Thank you!

www.joycewilde.com

Cover drawn by Rick Carter and designed by Heather Desuta.

ISBN-13: 978-0-9911-3160-0

ISBN-10: 0-9911-3160-6

First Printing: 2013

To that force which animates me,
gives me breath, gives me hope,
makes my heart beat and my soul sing...
Thank you. I am happy to contribute in this way.

Acknowledgments

When we follow our bliss,
we are met by a thousand unseen helping hands.
~ Joseph Campbell

A heartfelt thank you to my mother, Therese Brandl, my sisters, Linda Kallus and Barbara Denson, and my friend Sharon Lawrence for contributing to this work in so many ways. Thank you to John DeDakis for editing, and to Rich Zielinski for reviewing and giving me input -- and helping me get to the point!

Thank you to artist William Rock for helping me stay inspired, and to artist Susan Wagner for kindness and wisdom. Thank you to Acharya Fleet Maull for stimulating a new level of accountability. Thank you to Bob Cooper for various forms of support, and to my friend and webmaster Duane Bentzen. Thank you to Val Kucher, Betty Carter, Brynn Gminder, Fred Connors, Mary Cvetan, Mac Purvis III, and Michael Green for suggestions and ideas.

Thank you to Rick Carter for drawing the cover, and Heather Desuta for the design. I love it.

Thank you to Dr. Marshall Rosenberg. I benefitted enormously from almost a decade of nonviolent communication trainings and your compassionate viewpoint. I have much to share in these pages because of you.

Finally, thank you to Prem Rawat. I have sat quietly in meditation for an hour a day since June 2002. Before I met you I was a "human-doing," not a human being. It is from your teachings, and the silence, these understandings and this work has sprung.

Contents

Introduction

When everything seems to be going against you,
remember that the airplane takes off against the wind, not with it.
~ Henry Ford

I wrote this book because I've stayed organized (and therefore stayed sane) in a variety of settings using these five steps on a regular basis, and, as you will see, I like helping others. If you get stuck when you try to get and stay organized, this guide will help you understand and address the roots of your challenges, and demystify the process by providing simple yet effective guidelines to support you.

Who is this Book for?

If you're sick and tired of how disorganized your life is, this book is for you. Are you ready to make lasting changes, and not just *think* about making changes? If so, then this book is definitely for you. Whether you're new to organizing, or have tried multiple organizing systems, or already have the "bones" of organization in place, if you're ready to make some new lifestyle changes in the way you organize, this is the book you need.

The five steps contained in this guide work whether you're male or female, right-brain creative, left-brain logical, or a very balanced right-left brain person.

It's maddening to be disorganized -- to want or need something but you can't find it. If you hate organizing but want to be organized because you see how it would help you at work with your projects, or at home with your family -- these steps may be just what you've been looking for.

This book is for people who are sick of *trying to be* organized and who are tired of *failing* at being organized, and who don't want to be *temporarily* organized. It's for people who want to be organized as a *way of living.* It's for those who are open to understanding that the key to success in getting and staying organized is to *consistently apply* what you read here.

> *The time to repair the roof is when the sun is shining.*
> ~ John F. Kennedy

Why do These Five Simple Steps Work?

Because they are guidelines that are easy to remember and broad enough to be inclusive, yet they are specific enough to be effective. You tailor-make them to suit you and your circumstances. Adapt them to fit your lifestyle. They are designed to be used throughout your daily activities no matter where you are or what you're doing.

The steps are easy to remember, and they work whether you're really busy, or when you have more time on your hands. They can be used in any situation you need to physically organize -- whether it's your business, office, home, car -- or your move across the country. They also work in situations where you need to mentally and emotionally get yourself organized.

The value of embracing these five steps as a habitual way of living is that you don't have to think about organizing, you focus instead on the projects and activities in your life.

> *All instruction is but a finger pointing to the moon....*
> ~ Zen Saying

The moon is your projects, what you want to get done. Organizing gets it done.

More About the Five Simple Steps

These steps don't have to be done in any particular order (although sometimes it is wise to do so). They are meant to be applied as needed, and repeated as often as necessary. They work in both the physical and electronic worlds.

These five steps are similar to the premise that to lose weight and keep it off, you do so by making a variety of positive lifestyle changes, not by dieting. They are deliberately oversimplified and in many ways similar to the basic guidelines of life: Exercise daily and drink water, eat veggies, get enough rest, and when in doubt, be kind.

It is great boldness to dare to simplify oneself.
~ Marie de Beausacq

Hate Organizing But Want to be Organized?

By using these guidelines and answering the questions presented, you'll have a greater understanding of the root causes of your challenges to get and stay organized, and therefore you will become more emotionally and mentally organized.

Increasing your awareness and developing new habits result in an internal and external transformation as you learn to connect your heart with your head (Step One), and your head with your hands (Step Two).

Order is not pressure which is imposed from without
but an equilibrium which is set up from within.
~ José Ortega y Gasset

This Guide is Best Used as a Workbook

This book is meant to be read, digested, and used a little at a time, over time. However, the five steps can be grasped easily, and implemented right away.

I often hear people say, in exasperation, "I don't know where to begin!" As Pema Chödrön says, "Start where you are." Now is the best time.

~ JOYce

Chapter 1

The Psychology of Organizing

Identify your problems but give your power and energy to solutions.
~ Tony Robbins

If you've tried to get and stay organized, and failed, yet you've read books and articles and listened to people talk about getting organized, these may be some of the reasons why:

- You focus on reading organizing books, rather than applying what's in them -- partly because the information in them is too complicated.

- Books on how to organize tell you what to buy to get organized -- and then you have to deal with all the new stuff you bought (on top, of course, of what you already have).

- Information about organizing focuses on the concept of getting organized -- and makes you excited about being organized as if there's an end point. Rather, it needs to be understood that organizing is a process that is managed best with ongoing lifestyle habits.

- Organizing books have great ideas, however, you're unable to apply them because the emotional and mental roots of the problem haven't been recognized and addressed.

Identifying the Roots

"I want my brother to see how messed up I am because of what happened to us! But I hate that I'm a hoarder. Please help me!" Jocelyn's strained voice conveyed her frustration as we surveyed her overpacked house. She kicked some of her belongings out of the way and muttered under her breath, "This will never change; there's something wrong with me."

To her credit, Jocelyn quickly identified the roots of her current situation and openly shared them. Those two initial processes can be very challenging. Next, for her to do something different, she needed to learn something different. Then, she needed to consistently put new behaviors into action.

The Power of Labels

"I do not care for the term hoarder, and do not use it" I said to Jocelyn. "The last thing a person who's struggling needs is a label that judges or shames them. Instead, I find ways to support people when they feel stuck -- and I use compassionate communication. I'm guessing that you are very sentimental and have trouble letting go."

Jocelyn's face lit up, "I am! So, you understand. Thank you!"

There is a wisdom of the head, and... there is a wisdom of the heart.
~ Charles Dickens

Getting to the Roots

Organizing will probably fail if it only addresses the symptoms of the disorganization and doesn't get to the root causes. It's like mowing the dandelions from your yard; they'll grow back. To make effective and lasting changes, you need to pull them out by the roots.

In the same way, your physical surroundings are a reflection of your mental and emotional processes.

You don't need intensive psychotherapy, just a piece of paper and a pen -- or a friend or family member with whom you can speak openly, and the ability to be honest with yourself. Answer the questions below -- and answer quickly -- with the first thing that comes to mind.

Honesty, Privacy and Safety

The reason you need to answer quickly is that otherwise your mind will edit and put in the politically correct answer. It's also important that you can answer without fear of someone else judging you, so if you're writing, make sure your answers are done privately and you can store them in a safe place. Or shred them after writing and learning from them. It's really important to make sure no one will find your answers and embarrass you or give you unpleasant feedback. Also, don't worry if anyone else would agree with you. Your perception is your reality.

Ask Yourself:

- When I was growing up, were my parents/caregivers organized? (Write about each, separately.)
- If no: Why weren't they?
- If yes: Was it in a balanced way -- or was it overly organized/clean?
- What emotions did/does this cause in me?
- How did/do my caregivers treat my level of organization (duties, chores, housekeeping) as a child and as an adult?

Now, write or talk about anything else that comes to mind that's related. For example, if your parents/caregivers are still alive, has their level of organizing (and other dynamics related to organizing) changed? How do you feel about that?

The Power of Role Models

Role models -- especially in the family from which you came -- have strong influence. This influence should not be minimized. Role models are a powerful force in shaping behavior.

By looking at the family you came from and identifying the sources of your conditioning, you can create solutions for changing the parts of your life that aren't working. This isn't about blaming. It's about getting to the sources and acknowledging and understanding (and perhaps accepting and forgiving). Whatever happened to you, may not be your fault; however, it's your responsibility, if you want to change it.

If you're unsatisfied with your life and want to empower yourself, this is the approach that moves you from being disempowered to empowered. This process takes you from being a victim of circumstances to a "co-creator" in charge of your life.

If you cannot get rid of the family skeleton,
you may as well make it dance.
~ George Bernard Shaw

Going Toe-to-Toe with Your "Stuff"

Answering those questions and writing your story begins to put you in touch with the sources of the frequent and repetitive thoughts you experience and behaviors you carry out. These thoughts and behaviors either support you or sabotage you. You were taught by family members, friends, teachers, your culture, television, and the media (in its various forms). Now you need to decide what you want to think, how you want to behave, and what you want to create in your life.

It can be hard to look at your past. It can also be liberating -- if you're ready -- especially when you learn to accept and forgive. Usually people ignore the past because they don't feel equipped to deal with it. It seems too painful. You may not have the tools, resources, energy, encouragement or support. Maybe you don't want to take the time, or see the value in investing the time. Or perhaps you haven't yet had a guide to help you learn what shaped you and what motivates you. This book is that guide.

Be prepared at any moment to sacrifice what you are
for what you could become.
~ Charles Dickens

Ask Yourself:

- What's my motivation for wanting to get and stay organized?
- Has my ability to be organized changed over time?
- Why not leave things as is, why bother to organize myself better?
- Is there some payoff to staying disorganized?
- Is it possible I have anger, resentment or some other emotional blockages that need resolved in order to get and stay organized?

Write or tell someone a short summary -- as it relates to organizing -- of what happened to you, what it was like, and what you want to create in your life now. Talk about things like what you wish to release, grow beyond, let go of, come to terms with, or create.

Where equilibrium and harmony are realized to the highest degree,
heaven and earth will attain their proper order
and all things will flourish.
~ Confucius

There's Hope

By reading this and answering these questions, you'll understand the causes of your current situation. You'll also learn a more positive and productive way of perceiving the world and processing your mental, emotional and physical stuff. You'll learn to observe, acknowledge, and adjust your thoughts and behaviors.

Love many things,
for therein lies the true strength,
and whosoever loves much performs much,
and can accomplish much, and what is done in love is done well.
~ Vincent Van Gogh

Chapter 2

Step One: Let go. Simplify. Reduce the Flow in

Everything should be made as simple as possible, but no simpler.
~ Albert Einstein

I dropped out of college and took a three-month road trip to Southern California when I was twenty-one. Shortly before leaving Pittsburgh, Pennsylvania, I was packing for the move and consulted Mom: "What do I keep? What do I let go of?" I had no idea what life would entail.

She replied, "You'll get rid of some things and wish you hadn't, and keep some things and wonder why."

Mom's words of wisdom still ring in my head. I often share them along with, "There's no way to do this perfectly, unless you have a crystal ball."

If you *do* have a crystal ball, let's package it, shall we? We'll make a billion dollars. In the meantime, since human beings have not yet perfected technology that can predict the future, there's guesswork involved. That sounds obvious, but it's where people often get stuck. If perfectionism is what's causing this to be a challenging process, here's a tip:

Strive for excellence rather than perfection.
~ Joyce B. Wilde

There's just no perfect way to do this. It's a process of trial and error, of noticing and adjusting.

Processing vs. Organizing

There are two parts to organizing, the first part is processing. This is when you think about any given object (or idea, computer file, email, etc.) and decide whether you'll keep it and why.

The second part is organizing. This is the actual physical act of placing the object (or idea, computer file, email, etc.) somewhere.

> Example: In the case of time management,
> processing is deciding what you'll do,
> and organizing is grouping tasks together.

The Challenge of Processing

You'll typically come face-to-face with your attachment to things -- and the people, places and times they represent. Dealing with sentimental feelings is one of the reasons this first step can be challenging.

Human beings are somewhat like computers in the sense that to function most effectively, "updating the software" is necessary from time-to-time. Unlike a machine; however, updating requires time for a human being to mentally and emotionally adjust to the changes.

As you begin to process items, ask yourself these questions to get clear on why you have what you have, what it means to you, and what to do next:

Ask Yourself:

- Why am I keeping this item?
- Am I ready to let go?
- Do I really need this?
- Will I actually use it?

- Do I still *want* to own this item -- whether I actually need it or will use it -- or do I feel obligated?

> *The one who removes mountains*
> *does so by carrying away small stones.*
> ~ Chinese Proverb

Hanging On?

If you're having trouble letting go, as most folks do, some of the reasons you probably hang on to stuff include one or more of the following:

You don't want to face the decision. - You're afraid you'll need it someday. - You think you haven't gotten the value out of it. - It seems wasteful. - The item represents the love someone gave you -- or didn't. - The belonging symbolizes the connection you had, or wished you'd had, with someone. - The object reminds you of something you don't want to forget (or, ironically, something you *do* want to forget!). - You think that, "No one will love it as much as I do." - The item is connected with some unfulfilled wish or dream you have. - The object is part of someone else's unfulfilled wish or dream, for which you feel responsible. - You feel strong emotions (such as grief, guilt and shame) when letting items go. - You haven't yet given yourself permission to let go....

Sound familiar?

Trust Your Intuition

Learn to listen to -- whatever you call it -- your instincts, intuition, or inner wisdom, and cultivate a "head-heart balance." Pay attention to the little voice that tells you, *It's okay to let go of this now* -- or -- *I'm definitely going to need, want, or miss this later.*

The good news is, if you *do* let go of something you need, most things can be replaced. Be discerning and differentiate between those items that are generic and those items that have sentimental, or other value, and you definitely want to keep.

There comes a leap in consciousness, call it intuition or what you will,
and the solution comes to you and you don't know how or why.
~ Albert Einstein

If You Don't Let Go...

The problem with ignoring that little voice, or not trusting it, and keeping too much stuff is:

You can't find what you need when you need it. - You end up buying items you already own. - You feel overwhelmed and frustrated. - You feel overburdened and the situation seems hopeless. - You feel like you're being held back by your stuff. - You waste time looking for things you know are *somewhere*. - You're fatigued at the very thought of dealing with your stuff. - There's no room to put away what you used today because what you used yesterday is in the way. - You end up running late and you're pretty sure it has something to do with all this stuff.

Chip Away, Release, Update

A couple years after moving to Santa Monica, I took an art class to sculpt stone and chose a big rough piece of alabaster. The assignment was, "Find the form within the stone." I slowly, methodically chipped away. As I did, I began to create and release the form within.

I saw the angel in the marble and carved until I set him free.
~ Michelangelo

Letting go and simplifying are similar processes. As you begin to let go, you have the opportunity to release a new version of yourself. Let go of everything that isn't aligned with a current or future vision of you. To do this, bring yourself into the present moment and begin to connect your heart with your head.

Ask Yourself:
- Do I love this?
- Is this item relevant in my life, today, or does it represent a past version of me?
- Does this item still feel good to me?
- Could someone else use or enjoy this more than me?
- Can I give myself permission to let go?

Letting Go
Our principles are the springs of our actions.
Our actions, the springs of our happiness or misery.
Too much care, therefore, cannot be taken in forming our principles.
~ Red Skelton

Letting go of belongings helps you more clearly define who you are because your physical stuff is symbolic of your mental and emotional stuff. As you engage in this process you may find the need to let go of, or minimize nonproductive activities and toxic relationships. Give yourself space for the new you that's emerging. Processing and organizing can help you get in touch with, acknowledge and release outdated images of yourself, long-held habits, and limiting beliefs.

As you let go of your items, thoughts and feelings tend to get stimulated. Here are questions to help you get more emotionally and mentally organized. Be honest and gentle with yourself as you ponder and answer.

Ask Yourself:

- Am I having trouble letting go because I'm carrying a resentment, guilt, grief or shame?
- Do I need to mourn the loss of something?
- Is there someone to whom I need to make amends or with whom I need to speak?
- How do I want to feel?
- How do I create that feeling for myself?

Write or talk out a short summary in answer to one or more of these questions: Why do I have trouble processing my items and letting go? Or: Why is simplifying my life challenging for me? Or: I can let go and simplify. My challenge with organizing is:_____.

Handling Your Emotions

Answering the questions and telling your story will help you get clearer on the emotional and mental aspects of this process. Don't be surprised if you experience sadness, anger, frustration, irritability and other strong emotions. Be prepared to handle your emotions by talking about them, writing about them, or using whatever healthy ways you've found to manage your thoughts and emotions.

And if you can let go easily, wonderful! I've worked with people who joyfully embraced this process. One woman would exclaim, "Be free!" as she purged items.

What is man but his passion?
~ Robert Penn Warren

Keep Your Dreams

Gloria exclaimed, "Don't make me let go of my dreams!" shortly after we began working together. I reassured her that I wouldn't. Please understand that this letting go process helps you *create space* for your dreams; it isn't about throwing them away.

By being discerning as you let go, you are able to focus on what you really love and also grow and expand into new areas. A stronger and clearer *you* will emerge.

Note: If you consider yourself a collector -- keep the things you love. Find a way you can display and enjoy the items.

Cultivate Balance

"I hate that my mother has kept all this stuff!!" cried Tony as he haphazardly dumped the contents of a kitchen drawer into a big black trash bag.

There's a balance between keeping everything -- your dreams and the items you enjoy collecting -- and getting rid of everything, like "Throwing the baby out with the bathwater."

Throwing the entire contents of drawers into the garbage is a problem on a number of levels: You may unknowingly throw away valuable items. You may harm the environment by putting things into the trash that ought to be recycled; or you may have "throwing-away-regret" later.

In this letting go process, I encourage you to recycle, reuse, repurpose, re-gift, and donate. The last stop is the trash bin.

I love it, but I don't have a place to put it... I know! I'll re-gift it!
~ Naomi

Limit the Flow In

Recently my sister came to visit and gave me a computer screen cleaner. She watched with amusement as I stood with it in my hand. I was thinking, *Do I need this? I already have one at my desk, and a decorative backup screen cleaner sitting nearby. If I keep this, where will I put it?*

She asked me what I was thinking and I shared my thoughts with her. She told me about another professional organizer she watched go through the same process. A moment later I decided the screen cleaner would find a good home in my computer bag. Then next time I am out and about with my laptop, I will have a screen cleaner with me.

With everything that comes my way, I go through this process of deciding if things are the right fit for me; and if so, where they belong in my life. I encourage you to do the same. Be discerning. Whether it's a physical object, a new friend, or a volunteer opportunity; managing everything takes time.

Reduce distractions and focus on what *you* want to create in your life.

Linen requires too much of a relationship.
~ Catherine Peek

The Effect of TV

Television is a wonderful tool, and can have positive and negative effects. Programs about organizing may be helpful to you, or they may be misleading because they make it look like you wave a magic wand

and everything around you is organized in an afternoon. It isn't. If you rush it, it would be like trying to hurry when sculpting the stone. You would probably make a mistake and cut off a big piece and ruin it. Mentally and emotionally it could be devastating to rush this process. Let go of too much, too quickly, and it will likely cause undue stress. Remember: This is a *process*, not an event.

There's a time and place to wave a magic wand (which I'll talk about in Chapter 13), but magic wands are not helpful with the nitty gritty of physical organizing. Sometimes you just need to roll up your sleeves and *get to it.* That's the bad news. The good news is that in doing so, you empower yourself.

> *You'll never plow a field turning it over in your mind.*
> ~ Irish Proverb

Leaving California - "Do I love this?"

Twenty-six years after I arrived in sunny Southern California, I decided to leave. As I stood surveying the contents of my home, I decided to keep only what would be useful and practical, and what I truly loved. With each item I'd ask myself, "Do I love this?" and other questions that are listed in this chapter. Moving is a great time to take advantage of the change in your life and purge items.

Imagine a person with both arms full of big paper bags filled with groceries. If someone tries to hand them one more thing, they cannot gracefully accept it. If they try, they are in danger of dropping what they are already carrying. This is why it's important to learn to let go, simplify, and reduce the flow in. The difficulty can be that there's a gap in time between letting go of one thing and embracing the next. For ideas on how to handle this period of time, see Chapter 19. **Mind the Gap** will help you learn how to use mindfulness in this process.

The things that we love tell us what we are.

~ Saint Thomas Aquinas

Chapter 3

If Step One is Challenging

I know from experience that arbitrarily imposing
strict discipline on myself normally results in fits of rebelliousness,
followed by pangs of guilt and compulsive self-recrimination.

The above phrase in Fleet Maull's excellent book, *Dharma in Hell,* stood out to me. I pondered how perfectly he described the human condition, and how much it relates to organizing.

If Step One is challenging, make sure you're motivated by your own *positive* reasons. Otherwise, *negative* internal statements will probably erode your commitment. And negative prompts from someone saying, "You should..." may initially motivate you, however it's likely they will not sustain you over time. One way or the other, negative input typically causes resentments to build up, and will ultimately drain your energy.

Happiness doesn't depend on any external conditions,
it is governed by our mental attitude.
~ Dale Carnegie

Layers of an Onion

Think of the experiences of processing and organizing like peeling layers off an onion and then chopping it into sections. It requires patience -- and sometimes causes tears.

I've worked with folks who, in the middle of our organizing session, sat down in frustration and cried. I've assisted couples who yelled at each other. And I've helped families who lost their tempers and threw things.

Having worked in many crisis intervention situations in mental health settings and with law enforcement, I learned to stay calm and give plenty of time and space. So, I encourage you to be patient. Sometimes it is best to move along with "baby steps." When you begin to let go, it is common to encounter unresolved issues that you've been avoiding or have been too busy to deal with. Shame, guilt, grief and other emotions can get triggered. It's also common for people to be surprised and taken aback when their feelings get stirred up. They don't expect this to happen, so they aren't prepared for it.

Shame

"Oh, I feel terrible about that!" Judy blurted out as she picked up a little grey ornament on her windowsill. It looked as if she was being burned by a hot rock as she quickly placed the item back where she found it. She noticed me looking at her quizzically, and continued, "I was supposed to follow through with something for the couple who gave me that and I never did. They live nearby and I'm always afraid I'm going to run into them! I'm so ashamed I didn't follow through. What do I *do*?"

We talked about it and I suggested, "Why not write them a short letter of explanation and apology?" My client was elderly, and, though she had their email address, she was not very Internet savvy. She had the home address and phone number. I suggested, "If you send a letter rather than make a phone call, they can think about what you write and reply if they want. Either way, you'll know you've done what you can -- and you won't have to duck behind an aisle if you run into them at the grocery store."

Judy thought that was a good suggestion and decided once she'd sent the letter she'd let go of the trinket they'd given her. She felt it was time to take action on that unresolved situation in her life.

Don't be surprised if you encounter feelings of shame when you begin to process and organize your belongings. It's common. You'll probably remember things you meant to do, or don't feel good about. If you can address it sooner than later, please do it; if not, attend to it when you can.

If you have to eat crow, do it while it's still warm.
~ Anonymous

Guilt

Felicia exclaimed, "I can't let go of this ashtray, grandmother gave it to me! The problem is -- if I'm absolutely honest -- I *hate* this thing! And I hate that I'm the family member who's obligated to hang onto all this stuff. I'm sick of it and it's such a relief to be able to admit it to someone who isn't going to make me feel bad!!"

I'm honored when people feel comfortable sharing their innermost feelings. They know I won't judge them. As you go through this process, it's important to be able to sort it all out -- whether by writing and/or talking. If you can manage without assistance, that's great. If not, find a friend, family member, or professional who can help you.

Sometimes the challenge is grief when you let go...
and guilt when you say no.
~ Joyce B. Wilde

If it's hard for you to face all of this because of the thoughts and emotions that get stirred up, you're not alone. Most people put on a social mask and don't talk about their struggles. The solution is to find some safe ways to acknowledge what you're feeling, and get support and guidance. Read more about the value of hiring a professional in Chapter 20.

Grief

"I'm moving across the country and need some advice, Joyce. I can't let go of a CD dad gave me a few years ago. Honestly, I don't really like the CD; I only listened to it once, but he died recently and it's too painful to let go."

We talked about it, and Diana decided to put the CD in a pile of items she intended to take with her. A few days later she picked it up and thought about it again. She recognized it was the love she has for her father she wants to keep, and that resides in her heart. Then she was able to let go of the CD.

Memories don't take up any physical space,
but they do take up a lot of psychic space.
~ John DeDakis

John is a novelist and veteran journalist, and has an astute understanding of grief and the human condition. The context for his quote is what John said he learned when he finally decided to sell the electric train set his parents -- now dead -- gave him for Christmas more than fifty years ago. He made this insightful comment recently while we were working on our book *Healing from Grief.* If you're struggling with grief, I not only suggest reading our book when it comes out, but also John E. Welshons' excellent book *Awakening from Grief: Finding the Way Back to Joy.*

I find Welshons' viewpoint very insightful. In addition to fully exploring the subject of grief, he also writes about the related experience of pleasure. He explains how happiness is, at its essence, an internal experience.

When people are grieving they sometimes seek external stimulation -- for example, through shopping -- to stimulate the internal sensation of happiness. I'll talk more about the dynamics of pleasure and shopping in a little bit, but first, as you process and organize your items, I suggest you give yourself the time and space -- and permission -- to process shame, guilt, and grief.

Uncover, discover, discard.
~ Anonymous

Ask Yourself:

- Do I feel ashamed, guilty, or grief-stricken when I think about letting go?
- What are the next steps for me to address these unresolved emotions?
- Would speaking with a counselor benefit me?
- Am I receiving support in my relationships around these issues?
- What have I done in the past that's worked?

Connecting the Heart and Head

If you're having trouble with Step One it's sometimes because your heart and head aren't yet entirely connected. You can sometimes see evidence of this disconnect in your life, when what you want to create isn't aligned with your actions.

Happiness is when what you think, what you say,
and what you do are in harmony.
~ Mahatma Gandhi

When what you want in your life isn't in sync with what you do, there are usually roots in your past, and there is often some external evidence. An example of this is the phenomenon called "depression-era mentality." If your parents or grandparents went through The Great Depression of the 1930s, you may have trouble letting go of belongings because of the emotional trickle down effect. This is a fear that resources are limited -- especially in a time of shortage -- and demands that nothing be wasted. As a result, you might think you'll need things or haven't gotten the value out of them -- yet you know those fears are unfounded and come from something you were taught, and not really applicable today.

Pleasure

And then there is the opposite end of the continuum, when people easily throw things away and buy new belongings without much thought or awareness of the choices they're making or the impact those choices have.

Often the reason that people shop is to stimulate feelings of happiness. There's brain chemistry research that explains it: Chemicals, including dopamine (which causes people to feel good), are stimulated by shopping.

The solution? Learn to access positive feelings without external stimulation.

Pleasure that springs from inside your core is always accessible to you. Whereas, good feelings that are triggered by some stimulus on the outside can cause an attachment to the person, object, or situation. This is a temporary state and needs to be repeated to be experienced again. This feeling that's dependent on something is a very risky way to fill your happiness quotient. If you love shopping, you may have created "shopping-dependent happiness" in your life.

Don't mistake pleasure for happiness.
They are a different breed of dogs.
~ Josh Billings

If you're ready to limit the flow in, you'll probably need to find ways to access that feeling of pleasure that resides inside of you. Meditation can be useful and powerful. However, if you don't like meditating or can't sit still, perhaps try a "working meditation" like gardening, or walking. Or consider doing some type of creative activity; just be careful that it doesn't become an excuse to buy more stuff.

In certain cultures people equate more stuff with being happy. In other cultures, people have very little, materially, yet often have more time to enjoy themselves and their families.

If an Arab in the desert were suddenly to discover a spring in his tent,
and so would always be able to have water in abundance,
how fortunate he would consider himself;
so too, when a man who... is always turned toward the outside,
thinking that his happiness lies outside him,
finally turns inward and discovers that the source is within him.
~ Soren Kierkegaard

Ask Yourself:

- Do I shop to feel happy or fill a void?
- Am I willing to modify this behavior?

- What can I do other than shop?
- Would support and assistance be helpful?
- In what forms would I accept help to address this dynamic?

More About Shopping

If you are a do-it-yourselfer and want to start addressing this challenge on your own, begin to pay attention to how you feel when you **want** something, and how your feelings shift once you **have** it. The dynamics around wanting and having are two very different experiences.

I was able to stop compulsive shopping by doing the following things:

- Remembering that I wasn't necessarily *accomplishing* something when I was shopping.
- Observing with enjoyment the clothing other people wear without feeling I need to own it (after all, I can't see it once it's on me!).
- Reducing the frequency of going to the mall, and the amount of time I spent there.
- Asking myself "If I buy this, where will I put it?"
- Waiting 24 hours before making a purchase.
- Meditating.

I learned to operate in the grey area, also. Sometimes people struggle with limiting the flow in because of all-or-nothing thinking. Don't deny yourself, just learn to think it over. Be discerning. Begin to modify your behavior and decrease your purchases.

One of my clients said, "Just remember, whatever you have, has you." If you have a boat, you need to care for the boat. It is sometimes better to have a friend with a boat.

Again, this is like learning to make your entire lifestyle a healthy one, without extremes; rather than dieting and feeling deprived, then resorting to binge eating. I encourage you to start with small steps in the direction you want to go, and seek the middle way.

Balance is best in all things.

~ Homer

Chapter 4

Step Two: Create Categories. And Use Them

Nothing is particularly hard if you divide it into small jobs.
~ Henry Ford

I encourage you to cultivate living in the present and connecting your head with your hands, and you will have success with Step Two. Handle objects and ideas with deliberation and purpose and decide where to put them. In the computer this is done by creating aptly named folders and documents. Get in the habit of asking yourself:

Where will I look for this next time? - or -
Where will I look for this, first, when I need it again? - and -
What is the broad category in which this item belongs?
- then (if necessary) -
What is the more specific category in which this item belongs?

With each of these questions, use what comes to mind first and without second guessing or editing your answers. And if nothing comes to you, take a moment, breathe, and get clear inside yourself. Then try again.

Next, establish physical boxes, baskets, trays, or bins where you'll put items. One advantage is you will see how many of each you have. We're a consumer society; it's common for people to be surprised at the number of plastic bags, tools, or makeup they have.

Do What Works for You

Don't worry about what someone else might do. Create your own methods and find your own way.

And don't get concerned if your system doesn't make sense to anyone else (unless they use or evaluate it). If it makes sense to you, do it -- rather than trying to fit yourself to someone else's idea of how things should be.

Think of this in the same way you answer security questions. For example:

* Who was your favorite teacher?
* What was the first thing you learned to cook?
* What was the first film you saw in the theatre?
* What was the name of your most beloved pet?

Though there may be multiple answers to these, one answer usually comes to mind the strongest. Though it's a little bit of a different dynamic, it's similar in that you want to use the *first thing that comes to mind* without hesitating or second guessing.

Don't Mix Things - Put "Like with Like"

"What's in this box?" I asked Kat as we organized the top floor of her 1880s Bed and Breakfast Inn. She peered into the container and replied "It's just a bunch of miscellaneous items." I responded, "There's really no such thing."

She looked at me quizzically. I said, "May I hazard a guess at where some of the items could go?"

She agreed, and I pulled out sticky notes, pens, paperclips and a stapler, and asked, "Do these go in your office, perhaps in a desk drawer?"

Kat nodded. And I continued, "Here are a couple screwdrivers and a hammer. Do they go in the garage? I think you've got a tool box in there, yes?"

She nodded again. Just then I saw the lightbulb come on over Kat's head. She understood what I meant by "Create categories."

The general category was the room, the more specific category was the place in the room. And sometimes it gets more specific than that. But to the extent you can, keep it simple. Generally speaking, the death to organizing is mixing things. The solution is to create clear categories. And then use them consistently.

If you're still confused or struggling to create categories, here's a list of questions.

Ask Yourself:
- Does this belong at work or home?
- In what room?
- In what area, closet, cupboard or drawer?
- Does this belong in my car?
- Does this belong to someone else, or need to go somewhere else?

Start with the general placement and then move to the more specific one -- I'll talk about that in Chapter 6.

Be Creative, Use What's On Hand First

When I was a young girl, my parents gave my sisters and me each a Barbie doll and a case, Barbie doll clothes, and a Ken doll. This was in the mid-1960s, and either the makers of Barbie didn't yet make all the accessories or my family couldn't afford them, so we girls created Barbie doll villages by scouring the family house: A shoe box and washcloth became a bed with blanket, a big ashtray became a jacuzzi they'd sit in during a Saturday night party; and Trolls became children for the Barbie doll couple.

How does this relate to organizing? When I work with people I always take the approach of using what's on hand, first. In other words, I *don't* encourage you to buy containers -- or anything -- until you need to. Remember, Step One is about letting go and simplifying, not about buying a lot more stuff (plus, until you know exactly what categories you'll need, you won't know). As you begin to organize, you'll need some basics, but most everybody has those items on hand. I'll cover those items in Chapter 8.

As you begin the process of organizing, you'll be surprised what you find and how easily items can be re-used and re-purposed. I often find that folks enjoy using belongings that were long forgotten, and giving them a second (or third) life; they like revisiting the memories of the people who gave them the gift, or the time period. Also, by using this approach I work within, and honor, people's budgets *and* I teach them how to be resourceful -- and a little greener.

A lively imagination is one of the best companions.
~ Frank Tyger

How to Create Categories - Example #1

I stood in Jonathan's home office; there were mountains of books lined up against each wall. I picked one up and asked, "Where will you look for this next time?"

He squinted at it for a moment and answered, "In my den, downstairs. I need to create an area for books about my various hobbies." I picked up another book and asked, "What about this one?"

He peered at it and pondered, then said, "That is for one of my businesses, so it would belong in here on that shelf over there."

By eliciting this information from him, we were able to "co-create" categories so he knew exactly where the different items would "live" from then on, in various places in his home, and home office.

Press on, nothing in the world can take the place of persistence.
~ Ray Kroc

How to Create Categories - Example #2

"What's that piece of paper?" I gently asked Ginny as she furtively stuck something in a cubby in her roll top desk. She was an elderly retired client, and we were working together in her home office, filing her paperwork.

She exclaimed, "I don't want to file that! It's from my grandson and I love it. I want to be able to find it and look at it."

The difficulty was that Ginny had many items she was sentimental about, and by tucking them away in various places, it caused her to feel upset and unable to find things. It also caused her to have a great deal of clutter and subsequently to feel overwhelmed.

We talked about it, and co-created a solution. We decided to make a file titled, "Things I enjoy." (Because that's what made sense to her.) Then every time we came upon some memento from family, friends, or her travels, she had a dedicated place to put these special items. On quiet Sunday afternoons she pulls out that file and enjoys looking through it --

and her desk and other living areas no longer have these items strewn about in various places.

Man does not simply exist,
but always decides what his existence will be,
what he will become in the next moment.
~ Viktor Frankl

How to Create Categories - Example #3

"Too many shoes!! Where do we put *all these shoes*?!" bellowed Antonio as we surveyed various parts of his home.

The answer: Get bins or racks and establish places where shoes will go. Each family member will probably be best served by having a "basic core" of shoes in their own closet. And then in the "shared spaces," make these areas obvious so everybody can easily participate.

If you're not bothered by visual clutter, have the bins or racks sitting out. If you are, establish areas inside closets, laundry rooms, etc. -- or find some lovely woven baskets with lids. You could also try shoe organizers that hang over the back of closet doors; they might just do the trick.

Often, shoes that are worn regularly (especially in a "no shoe" home) will be placed near the front or back door. (I'll talk more about the specific placement of items in Chapter 8). Use this same idea with establishing places for other household items.

Anticipate the difficult by managing the easy.
~ Lao Tzu

Chapter 5

If Step Two is Challenging

If you keep on doing what you've always done,
you'll keep on getting what you've always got.
~ W. L. Bateman

If Step Two isn't working for you yet, start paying attention to the way you're currently doing things. Begin to watch how you move through time and space.

Remember, implementing these guidelines is about making a change in your habits, not about just getting organized temporarily. Sometimes when you start to make changes it's as if you put a magnifying glass on the situation and it seems worse than it is, at least for a while.

Imagine a room that has been closed off and sat dormant for a long time. When you open the curtains and start to move things around, the dust gets stirred up and it seems worse for a while until things are rearranged and the dust settles. The same goes for when you start to observe your long-held thoughts and behaviors, and begin to change them.

If you try to categorize things and cannot figure out what the categories are, and find yourself with confused thoughts, and upsetting emotions, refer to Chapter 17 for some guidance and ideas.

More About the Effects of Television

Sometimes people have a hard time with Step Two because of organizing shows on TV. They make it look easier than it is. In real life it's labor-intensive to pick up one item at a time, stay focused, and decide what should be done with it. However, in the real world, this is what you need to do, until clear categories are created. This is how you get a system in place. It takes a little time and thought; that's the bad news. Once categories are established, it all becomes easier; that's the good news.

And in real life you've got to *remember and use* the categories you create; keep them going. Don't duplicate a category or you'll probably get confused and disorganized. Only create what you'll actually use. And practice continually making the connection between your head and your hands.

Notice and Adjust

> *Be here now.*
> ~ Ram Dass

Sometimes your brain is thinking about the past or the future -- "time traveling" -- and not truly experiencing the present moment. This is often why you don't use the categories you created.

Typically, you avoid the current moment -- you disconnect from it -- by using various methods like alcohol, food, sugar, caffeine, television, the computer, shopping, relationships, sex, etc. Even work can be used as a way for you to escape the present moment.

We *all* do this to some degree. So the question isn't *if* you're doing it, it's *how* you're doing it, how *much* you're doing it, and to what degree it's causing a problem with staying organized. The solution is to notice and adjust. Notice the disconnect and gently bring yourself back into the present moment.

And, please don't judge yourself harshly or beat yourself up. This just creates a new set of problems.

Again, learn to gently refocus when you realize you've gotten a little off track. Repeat this process as often as needed. Some people call it *mindfulness*. One definition of mindfulness is, "A mental state achieved by focusing one's awareness on the present moment, while calmly acknowledging and accepting one's feelings, thoughts, and bodily sensations."

Cultivating mindfulness can help you stay organized in general, in particular with putting things in categories, and using the categories you create.

Minimize Multi-tasking

Multi-tasking is overrated. It can make it much more challenging to be organized. In fact, you don't actually multi-task, you quickly switch tasks, sort of ignore one task momentarily and rapidly toggle back and forth, mentally, because your mind can hold only one thought at a time.

The solution: learn to focus, and effectively single task rather than multi-task. As often as you can, practice doing one thing at a time and put as much of your presence, your awareness, into that one thing.

We're encouraged to multi-task because it's supposed to make us get more done, quicker. Often when we move faster we actually end up making more mistakes, because distractions can cause mistakes. By slowing down and bringing your full attention to each task, you will actually get more done. By spending time, you will save time.

To do two things at once is to do neither.

~ Seneca

Side Benefits to this Process

By practicing mindfulness, you'll find you won't lose and misplace things as much. You may also find that you stop yourself from getting into accidents and creating other unnecessary problems. It is well known that momentary distractions cause many car accidents.

Practice staying in the present moment and it may help you save time, energy and money.

If you struggle with multi-tasking versus mindfulness, and would like to experience being more in the present moment, I recommend reading books by authors Eckhart Tolle, Pema Chödrön, and Thich Nhat Hanh.

Diminishing Returns

Don't engage in processing and organizing your items and creating new categories unless you have the energy and focus to do so. And stop before you get into diminishing returns.

When organizing, prepare your mindset: Get ready and willing to deal with things head-on rather than just sticking things anywhere because you can't deal with them. You probably place objects where it's convenient when you're feeling under-motivated, overwhelmed or overtired. The solution is to create clearly-defined categories when you have the energy, and then use them consistently.

Again, pay attention to what works for you -- in terms of the time you spend and the strategies you employ -- rather than some idea of what you *should* do.

Here's to the crazy ones. The misfits.
The rebels. The troublemakers.
The round pegs in the square holes.
The ones who see things differently.
They're not fond of rules.
~ Steve Jobs

Chapter 6

Step Three: Work from General to Specific

The best time to plant a tree was 20 years ago;
the second best time is today.
~ Confucius

"I just spent two hours organizing this drawer, how will I ever get the whole house organized?!" Merri exclaimed in despair as we began to work together. With that one phrase, she reinforced the importance of organizing from general to specific, from macro projects to micro tasks.

As we worked together, I saw what Merri meant. It was evident she would become so focused on one small project she would quickly lose sight of the big picture. One day we began organizing her garage. I watched as she started with the larger focus on getting the "bones" of organization in place, and then she'd forget and begin to hyper-focus on one particular area. Since we'd talked about it and agreed that's what would benefit her, I gently redirected her back to the big picture.

I have seen that hyper-focusing is a somewhat common phenomenon, and one of the primary reasons people have trouble getting organized and staying organized. Be gentle with yourself. Pay attention to what's happening, and remember:

Notice and adjust.
~ Merri

Overwhelm

I chose the Confucius quote to begin this chapter because often when people start the process of organizing, they throw their hands up in despair and exclaim, "I should have done this 20 years ago!" It's helpful to acknowledge that thought, process it to the extent you need to, and then *begin to take constructive action* by using the five steps described in this book.

What's done is done; you are where you are now. If you find your negative self-talk is getting in the way, please turn to Chapter 17.

There is some magic in *getting into action*. Taking constructive action and physically changing your environment with a well-thought-out strategy helps you actually see that you're moving forward, not just *thinking* about moving forward or *talking* about moving forward.

As Julie Cameron, author of *The Artist's Way*, says,
The act of motion puts us into the now and helps us to stop spinning.

Broad Categories

When organizing, start with broad categories. For example, when you come upon papers that need to be filed, as I talked about in Step Two, ask yourself, what room do these belong in? In what file cabinet do they go? And then when you are filing the papers, put all of one company's information into one repository, to begin with, only sort into subcategories as needed. You can get more precise when, and if, you want or need to.

Getting too precise too quickly can cause problems, making it more difficult to find things. I encourage bulk organizing and -- to the extent you can -- keeping things streamlined and simple. You don't want to spend more time organizing than necessary.

Also, starting with broad categories and then moving to more specific ones will help counter the feeling of being overwhelmed. Especially if things have built up over time, and you are just beginning the process of decluttering and organizing, it's helpful to be aware of the importance of keeping an eye on the big picture.

Stay Where You Are

Staying in the area you're organizing is another strategy for keeping your eye on the big picture. Don't get distracted by other things. If you leave the area, for example, to take something from your home office to your kitchen, it is likely you will get sidetracked there, or on the way to, or from that area. I'll explain how to stay in the area you're organizing in Chapter 8.

Reminder: It's a Process

It does not matter how slowly you go so long as you do not stop.
~ Confucius

In the Western world we are taught to always get to the proverbial finish line. Organizing is much more Eastern in that respect because it's an ongoing process.

Developing new habits takes time, effort, awareness, and a change in the underlying thought processes that drive behaviors. It takes a while to get the hang of something new, then over time it becomes easier and somewhat automatic, like riding a bike.

If you feel overwhelmed, you're not alone, please know that other people are feeling the same way and having the same struggles. People tend to hide behind their polite social mask and not divulge that they are struggling. It's common for folks to feel overwhelmed in the beginning of an organizing project, because there's so much to sort out, initially. Often people have no idea where or how to begin.

My Grandpa's House

My Grandpa was a bricklayer; he built houses. I love the analogy of that work as it applies to organizing. You clear the foundation, decide what you're going to create, and then put one brick at a time firmly in place.

I recently learned that Grandpa built his home from bricks that were left over from other jobs. It's a beautiful house; of course it's one of a kind. He thought it through and used all these different colored bricks in a clever strategy. You'd think it was deliberately done, and not made with "leftovers."

Do something every day to move yourself forward
and nothing to set you back.
~ Joyce B. Wilde

To Increase Your Motivation

Let's say you need to organize your spare bedroom (or any room or area). Start with a general decluttering first, rather than focusing on one box of items that needs to be sorted out.

What I mean by "a general decluttering" is: remove the easy and obvious items first. Carry out tasks and actions that will give you a visual impact. By taking this strategy, you'll feel more motivated and energetic when you return to the room or area because *you'll see your progress*.

If you spend a lot of time on one small project, your progress will not be as apparent and you'll likely feel demotivated when you return to work on the room next time.

As human beings,

our greatness lies not so much in being able to remake the world...

as in being able to remake ourselves.

~ Mahatma Ghandi

Exceptions

"Those really bug me because my ex-boyfriend gave some of them to me." Wendy pointed at a large stack of CDs in the corner and sighed. "I just recently started a new relationship and hate looking at those."

We were decluttering and organizing her living room, and I suggested she take a small block of time and review the CDs. Wendy expressed a great sense of relief as she put the unwanted music in a cardboard box, which we positioned by the front door so she would remember to take it out of her home (you'll learn about creating visual cues in Step Five). She wasn't bothered by visual clutter; if she was, I would have suggested we take it out to her car (and listed it on her calendar. You'll also learn about this in Step Five).

Putting ex-boyfriends aside, sometimes music gets stale and it's important to take time to remove the things that no longer resonate -- or perhaps they are no longer the current version of you (this may include clothes, shoes, hats, scarves, jewelry, books, etc.).

At the center of your being you know who you are

and you know what you want.

~ Lao Tzu

I suggest, however, that you keep an eye on the time when working on micro tasks, maybe only spend ten to 30 minutes on them. Some people like to set a timer to help them remember to stop; other people prefer to listen to their internal clock. If you *don't* limit the time you spend, it could backfire. You may end up in despair, like Merri, whose story I shared at the beginning of this chapter.

Other Exceptions

When beginning a project, people will often ask me where to start. I suggest you begin with what bothers you the most, what is easiest or most obvious, or what's most problematic or urgent. Some people are bothered by visual clutter, others aren't. You may wish to begin with what would make a difference in your relationship. If, for example, your partner is bothered by visual clutter and you aren't, and you want to relieve their discomfort, do something that would address that issue.

An example of working on a specific task is coming upon a stack of unpaid bills. Recently I was working with a client who discovered her electricity was going to get shut off if she didn't pay the bill. This is a worthy reason to set aside the big picture and focus on a smaller project. It's a more specific task, yet if it is essential to address something immediately, or if it is something that is really bothering you, go ahead and do it -- especially if it can be done quickly. Just remember and keep an eye on how much time you're spending.

Increased Awareness and Sensitivity May Occur

When you declutter and organize a space, you may start to become more aware of what's around you and how it's affecting you. It's good news and it's bad news. As layers of stuff are removed, typically you become more sensitive to what's in your immediate environment -- things you have been blocking out of your awareness. Then the items that bother you can be more readily identified and dealt with. You can more easily pare down to the items that you really love -- have "good energy" for you -- and with which you want to surround yourself.

I encourage simplifying your life and surrounding yourself with the things you really love. I'll talk more about this in Chapter 8.

Only in growth, reform, and change,
paradoxically enough, is true security to be found.
~ Anne Morrow Lindbergh

Chapter 7

If Step Three is Challenging

Out of clutter, find simplicity. From discord, find harmony.
In the middle of difficulty lies opportunity.
~ Albert Einstein

If working from general to specific is challenging for you, you may wish to enlist the help of a friend, family member, or professional, until you get the hang of it. It's sometimes very difficult to see yourself, your behavior and choices. In Step Three you need to keep an eye on the big picture, and, without input, you may not even be clear on what the big picture is!

Ask Yourself:

- Am I having trouble knowing how to work from general to specific?
- Am I feeling challenged with where to begin?
- What is the most problematic part of the area I want to organize?
- If I could wave a magic wand and create my ideal scenario, what would it look like?
- Am I willing to do what it takes to make that happen?

Honesty is the Best Policy

Step Three asks you to take responsibility and be honest with yourself. Do you really want to live in an organized way? Because if someone else wants you to do so, but *you* don't, you'll sabotage the process just to get them off your back.

And here's something to think about -- whatever has happened to you that created the dynamic of disorganization you're experiencing may not be your fault, but if you want to change it, you need to take responsibility. There are some things we can delegate, however, *nobody* can get you organized but you. That brings up the next set of questions. There may be some underlying resistance that's in your way.

Ask Yourself:

- Do *I* want to get organized or does *someone else* want me to get organized?
- Do I blame my lack of organization on someone else? (Be honest.)
- Why?
- And if so: How can I change that dynamic?
- How could I benefit by changing the way I'm operating?

I once read that as a plane travels from destination to destination it's off course something like 90% of the time. The plane just continues to make small course corrections. To work from general to specific, it is important that you pay attention to your behaviors and make small corrections as you go. Remember: notice and adjust. It may also take dealing with your *Schweinehund*.

Schweinehund

A German acquaintance once told me that when he tried to get himself to do something he didn't want to do, he could feel a *Schweinehund* sitting on him. *Schweinehund* is German for "pig dog." One of the definitions is, "One's inner resistance against making an effort." It's some of what's behind the joy of resisting. It's that defiant part of you that says:

Don't have to, ain't gonna.
~ Jackie

I suggest you get to know your inner *Schweinehund* and befriend it rather than fight against it. Fighting takes too much energy -- and you want to reserve your energy for the tasks at hand.

One strategy I encourage is to remind yourself how good you'll feel when the task or activity you're resisting is done. Or tell yourself you'll do the task or activity for only ten or twenty minutes. Usually once you've started you can stay with it much longer. Find a way to move beyond the "Get started with it already!" hurdle, and then usually the task isn't as bad or as hard as you think.

Celebrate any progress. Don't wait to get perfect.
~ Ann McGee-Cooper

Pat Yourself on the Back

And when you're done, pat yourself on the back, and revisit the task another day. It's important to take time and recognize your effort in some way.

It's always fun when someone else recognizes your efforts -- and it may be helpful to tell others about what you're doing and enlist them in your process -- however, don't wait for their praise. I learned the value of this many years ago when I started a new job and the woman I replaced told me, "Get in the habit of patting yourself on the back." She warned me that the boss wasn't very good at doing that.

It was excellent advice; I have followed it ever since and it has kept me in good stead. So, I encourage you, find some way to reward yourself for a job well done.

Ask Yourself:

- Am I disappointed when I do things and others don't acknowledge my efforts?
- Am I expecting others to provide rewards?
- Am I willing to modify my expectations and provide my own rewards?
- What are three things I could do to reward myself when I carry out a difficult task?
- Can I think of some healthy activities that don't revolve around shopping and/or eating?

Like a Wave

I find that there's a normal flow with the buildup of needing to organize. For example, sometimes you're really busy, or you'd rather be doing something else. Then you start to get uncomfortable. The filing is stacking up. Here and there things are getting cluttered. It's kind of like a wave building to its peak. Pretty soon you can't stand it anymore and you need to get into action to remedy the situation.

Sometimes when clients contact me for organizing assistance, it seems like they've gotten to this point. Things have been put off and built up, and they just can't stand it any longer.

Smile, breathe and go slowly.
~ Thich Nhat Hanh

Book Recommendation

If you find that you're continuing to stay stuck, Krishna Pendyala wrote an interesting book a couple of years ago: *Beyond the PIG and the APE: Realizing Success and True Happiness.* In it he aptly describes how we all "pursue instant gratification" (PIG) — which helps explain how folks sometimes end up with so much stuff. He says people attempt to "avoid painful experiences" (APE). If decluttering and organizing feel painful to you, this book may be a worthwhile read. Krishna's book was published in 2011 and is available on Amazon.com.

Real-life is dynamic. It's often shaky,
involving lots of movements off to one side and then to the other.
It's sometimes smoother, requiring fewer or smaller corrections.
But it's those little adjustments that are crucial.
~ Tom Morris

Chapter 8

Step Four: Keep Closest What You Use Most Often

Creativity is intelligence having fun.

~ Albert Einstein

Keep closest to you what you use most often, and what's convenient, useful, beautiful, feels good or makes sense. This sounds really obvious, I know! However, I often work with folks who are reaching around items and stepping past obstacles to get what they need and frequently use.

It seems like people worry more about the right way to do things, and how others do things, than what works best for them.

So, I encourage you -- pay attention to how you move through time and space. Position things for easy access; don't create areas that look good but there's no practical or comfortable way to use them. Create spaces that support you best, on all levels.

One caveat: Please don't infringe on shared spaces. Changes might benefit you, but will others be unnecessarily disturbed? Get their input before you proceed with your changes.

As you reevaluate the environment around you...

Ask Yourself:

- Is the placement of objects and items working for me and others?
- Am I open to trying something different?
- If yes: What might work better?
- What's holding me back from making changes?
- Do I need to bring something up at an office meeting or family gathering for input?

Paulo

"For five years I walked across the room of my vacuum cleaner shop to throw away things. One day my girlfriend, Stephanie, watched me. Then she moved the trash and recycle bins over near where my work station was located. I can't believe I never did that!" Paulo laughed, "Honestly, Joyce, it never occurred to me!!"

I thought that was a fabulous story for a variety of reasons. I admired Paulo's honesty, openness to change, and ability to laugh at himself. It was also a helpful story because years later when I began my organizing/coaching business, I became more aware of these personal dynamics in others.

Adapt to Changes

The art of progress is to preserve order amid change
and to preserve change amid order.
~ Alfred North Whitehead

Most of us don't like change; we gravitate toward the familiar, even if it isn't working well. And it can take a little time to adapt. If your environment isn't working for you, and you're open to changing it, one benefit is that your brain will thank you.

There's a lot of research showing the positive effects of stimulating the brain by making changes. And when we do things differently, it causes us to increase our mindfulness, because it keeps us more in the present moment, rather than operating on autopilot.

The Ham in the Pan

Do not let what you cannot do interfere with what you CAN do.
~ John Wooden

Have you heard the story about the young man who always cut off the end of the ham before cooking it? One day his mother came to visit and asked why he did this. He explained it was because that's what he'd always seen her do. She replied, "I did that to make the ham fit in the pan. Your pan is big enough."

I saw this kind of thinking in myself when I was just starting my organizing business. I attended a class and the instructor said that when seniors were downsizing it might be wise to reduce their china sets from ten or twelve to four or six. Honestly, it never occurred to me to break up a china set, keep some and donate the rest.

So, I encourage you to change things regardless of what you learned, if they're more effective for you another way. Make changes no matter *how long* you've been doing things. If they could work better another way, try that approach. Be open to change.

Review of the Steps so Far

As a review of what you've learned, and to demonstrate how it relates to Step Four:

Step One - Let go of items you don't need (I'll give you some specifics next), and reduce the inflow of items.

Step Two - Put things in categories (again, I'll give you some specifics next) asking yourself where you'll look for them next time you need them.

Step Three - Work from general to specific.

Step Four - As you position your items, think about the physical flow of your day, and put objects you use the most often where you'll be able to find and access them most easily. And keep at hand the items you enjoy and make your life wonderful. This is the most effective use of your prime real estate.

Remember to notice and adjust. It's common to move things around a little until you find what works best. And, just a warning, when you move one item, it may cause a chain-reaction where other items need to be relocated or slightly repositioned.

Don't be too timid and squeamish about your actions.
All life is an experiment.
~ Ralph Waldo Emerson

Physical Organizing - Approach #1

There are various ways to approach Step One. The first, and more thorough approach: Remove everything from an area and clearly identify what it is to be used for. Clean the space, then put the items back using the well-defined categories I talked about in Step Two. As much as possible, limit mixing items.

Only put into the area the items that you have determined it will be used for. Don't put additional items there because you don't know what to do with them; take a moment and think it through.

Ideally fill the space about two-thirds full. Do not fill it to capacity or it will quickly become overfull and disorganized.

Typically -- depending on the size of the area -- this process can take anywhere from less than an hour to several hours (or much longer, as it may need to be broken into various sessions).

Note: When cleaning the space, consider using natural products.
I recommend the book *Green Grandma's Vinegar Fridays*
by Hana Haatainen Caye.
Hana's book was published in 2011 and is available on Amazon.com.

Physical Organizing - Approach #2

If we don't change our direction,
we are likely to end up where we are headed.
~ Chinese Proverb

Another way to approach Step One is more superficial and faster. Clearly designate what a space will be used for, and just remove the items that don't belong.

For example, when processing and organizing your home office, quickly gather up the items that shouldn't be there. Then take cups and plates to the kitchen, tools to the garage, and so forth. Doing this simple removal may take just a couple minutes, or up to twenty minutes or so. I call it organizing in the "nooks and crannies" of life.

Read more about these two approaches, and a third approach, in Chapter 14.

Position Bags and Boxes Nearby

Whether you use Approach #1 or Approach #2, the most effective way to carry out Step One and Step Two is to position bags (plastic and paper, of various sizes) and boxes (plastic and cardboard, of various sizes) near the space you're working on so you don't need to leave it. Remember, the reason you don't want to leave the space is that you risk getting distracted and losing your focus.

Example

I'll describe how this works using a home office, assuming you also have an office outside your home:

Fill the various bags and boxes with items that belong in other places. Designate one box or bag for items that need to be returned to work, and one with items that need to go to your car (to get donated, or returned to the library, or a friend's house). Use another box or bag and put items in it that need to be returned to your kitchen, and one to put items that belong in another room in your home.

This is a very individual process and specifics will vary, depending on the items and where they belong. Have your recycle container, trash can, and shredder nearby.

I'll cover how you label these boxes and bags so they don't get mixed up, but first a little bit about shredding.

Shredder Tips

Action is the foundational key to all success.

~ Pablo Picasso

Either shred right away, or put a slight tear in the papers and put them in a container until you shred them. The tear will remind you they are to be shredded. If you put them in a bag or box, make sure and label it "Shred" or you may mistake it for recycle items.

Don't shred for too long as this may cause some shredding machines to overheat or wear out quickly. The best way to shred is for one minute, then let the machine rest for ten minutes. And if you don't have a shredder, there are a variety of places you can go to shred. There are also services that come and pick up the paperwork that needs shredded.

Labeling

When you begin to fill the boxes and bags, label them *temporarily* using sticky notes -- so you don't get them mixed up. This also saves time in that you don't have to think again about what's in any individual bag or box.

Use sticky notes at this stage because as you continue to purge, you may find you need much larger or smaller containers. The sticky notes allow you to switch boxes or bags easily. Further along in the process it's a good idea to label the containers permanently with a label or marker, so the notes don't fall off in transport or in storage.

Create Good Energy

In addition to positioning the practical items in effective places, surround yourself with the things you love and have good energy for you. Just be sure you keep it simple and don't overdo it.

> *If you know the point of balance, you can settle the details.*
> *If you can settle the details, you can stop running around.*
> *Your mind will become calm.*
> *If your mind becomes calm, you can think in front of a tiger.*
> *If you can think in front of a tiger, you will surely succeed.*
> ~ Mencius

Chapter 9

If Step Four is Challenging

Begin with the end in mind.
~ Stephen Covey

If Step Four is challenging, make sure you're doing what Stephen Covey suggested. Ask yourself, "If I could wave a magic wand, what would this look like?" That way you can get a clearer picture of your ideal circumstances. You may or may not be able to create *exactly* what you want, but at least you'll be clearer on the end goal.

Slow Moving Storm

"You should see my desk. Everything is piled in a heap. But you know what? I can find everything. So why should I take time getting organized?" Dan, the young scruffy editor smiled at me as he challenged my organizing guide concept. I replied, "I respect that. If you can find everything, then don't bother taking the time to get organized."

Dan tugged on his tie, grimaced, and said, "Well, to tell you the truth, sometimes I can't find something and it wastes a bunch of time and drives me crazy. I'm like a slow moving storm... Hmmm... Tell me about these five steps of yours...."

Time and New Habits

For many people, the time it takes to process and organize is the reason not to try something new. To initially get organized takes an investment in time. There's no way around it. It's up to you *how much* you are willing to invest.

On the other hand, when you spend time looking for things, you're wasting valuable time; and probably adding a few blood pressure points as well. Once you're organized -- and have clear categories in place, you just need to use them regularly. This is how you stay organized. These categories create your workflow systems.

Remember, the reason I teach organizing as five habit-forming steps is so you don't even have to *think* about organizing. You will simply focus on what interests you.

There is always enough time. It's how you choose to spend it. With organizing you *spend time to save time* (and energy and money and aggravation). It's an investment in yourself and your *quality of life.*

If you're still feeling challenged, I encourage you to hang in there and read to the end of this guide and answer all of the questions that are presented.

Fall seven times, stand up eight.

~ Japanese Proverb

Ask Yourself:
- Do I understand and accept that processing and organizing initially take an investment of time, energy and money?
- Am I willing to make those investments?
- Am I willing to try something different than I've been doing?
- Do I know exactly what I want to create?
- If no: Would it be helpful to talk it through with someone?

Current Version of You

Sometimes people have trouble with Step Four because they're struggling to be clear with the current version of themselves. For example:

- You're an empty nester now. You've defined yourself as a parent until now, and you're not as active in that role anymore.
- You've switched careers and are getting older and no longer identify with the part of you that thought or imagined you'd go in a different direction than your life is currently taking you. For example, you thought you'd be an artist, but right now you're a teacher.
- You're retired and no longer define yourself as the job title you identified with for so long.
- Your longtime spouse has passed away and you're still living in the environment you created together.
- You inherited your parent's home and it represents *them* more than *you*.

You may be surrounded with stuff that doesn't represent who you are today. And it doesn't support the direction you want to go in the future, either.

To be yourself in a world that is constantly trying to make you something else is the greatest accomplishment.
~ Ralph Waldo Emerson

A Blast to the Past

Have you ever spent time with family (for example, during the holidays) and watched yourself regress and act like a teenager? Did you do this even though you were an adult in your twenties, thirties, forties, fifties, or beyond?

One time when I lived in Southern California, Mom came to visit. I picked her up at the Los Angeles airport in my recently purchased black MG Midget. As I raced up the Pacific Coast Highway, I noticed my driving and speech patterns changed from that of a responsible 32-year old, to what felt like a 17-year old teenager. It was something about the thrill of driving my new stick-shift while reconnecting with my mother.

By the look on her face, I realized I was making her nervous, so I settled down and drove slower and more safely. I paid attention to what I was thinking and saying and how I was behaving.

Though I'd seen myself engage in versions of this behavior before, it was the first time it was really obvious to me that I'd switched into a younger version of myself. (Note: It may be more apparent if you don't live near family and see them infrequently.)

As you become organized and create systems that keep you organized, develop an awareness of who you are at this time in your life.

Ask Yourself:

- Does my environment express the current version of me or an outdated version?
- Does my environment represent someone else?
- Am I willing to give myself permission to change?
- What's the best next step?
- What assistance and resources do I need?

Embrace Choosing

Taking time to develop new systems and habits, and updating to the current version of yourself involves a little bit of awareness, effort and patience.

It's helpful to embrace it all in the spirit of choosing rather than feeling you have to. It takes courage to deal with your stuff.

Optimism is an elected attitude, a form of emotional courage.
~ Julia Cameron

Chapter 10

Step Five: Create and Use Visual Cues

Some people regard discipline as a chore.
For me, it is a kind of order that sets me free to fly.
~ Julie Andrews

Cindy, my favorite teacher in grad school, was speaking to the class and as she did so, moved her ring from one finger to another. It was obvious, and one of the students inquired, "Why'd you do that?"

"Because I thought of something I need to do when I get home, and when I get there, I'll be reminded," she replied.

This visual (and tactile) cue is a great example of how Step Five works.

Cues

Cues can be very simple -- like positioning something somewhere, or using sticky notes. Or cues can be very sophisticated -- when you're using electronic devices. Whether they are simple or complex, Step Five is about learning to identify which ones work best for you, and how to use them on a regular basis.

Cues are about using the **more** cognizant part of your brain to help the **less** cognizant part of your brain. Or to state it another way, it's how you get the part of your brain that thinks about doing something to help the part of your brain that is focused elsewhere at the time the task is supposed to be done.

Human beings tend to be visual, so that's why I focus more on visual prompts. But if you're more responsive to reminders that use the other senses; develop for yourself auditory and tactile ones, for example.

Proactive vs. Reactive

Cues are empowering. When you integrate them into your life, they allow you to be proactive rather than reactive. It's truly a bummer, for example, to pay late fees.

Develop the habit of creating and setting prompts to tell you *what* you need to do. Place them *where* you will be reminded to do them, *at the time* when they need to be done. When you are too busy, and need to let things go -- then schedule time on your calendar to get back to those items.

Remember, these steps are deliberately generic and meant to be made into habits (frequently occurring behaviors) that support you. Only you know exactly what you need and when you need it.

> *You form habits and then habits form you.*
> ~ Joyce B. Wilde

Example

"Ben makes me crazy. He can never find his stuff in the morning! You wouldn't think it would be that hard, living in this tiny two bedroom apartment." Jessica was exasperated with her husband and looked puzzled as she spoke, scanning her home.

We talked about the flow of Ben's typical morning. He had a regular routine which ended in the kitchen, with breakfast. I asked if the kitchen would be a good place to position some type of container to put his hat, keys, and wallet.

Just then Ben walked in. I repeated the idea and asked him what he thought of it. In answer, he pointed to the top of the refrigerator. This was a good choice for two reasons, Ben was tall, and their two small children wouldn't be able to reach that high.

We found a basket and positioned it there. Ben uses it on a regular basis.

Jessica thanked me later, saying it works great. And Ben told me he feels relieved that he has one specific place to put his items. He said that strategy allows him to leave for work on time, and reduces his stress.

For the first twenty-five years of my life, I wanted freedom.
For the next twenty-five years, I wanted order.
For the next twenty-five years, I realized that order is freedom.
~ Winston Churchill

Do it Now

Part of Step Five is doing something as soon as you think of it. Record it in some way, somewhere -- as soon as possible. Don't try to hold things in your head to do later; this can create stress.

Step Five is not just about creating strategies for support, it's about creating methods that increase your follow through and accountability. Very often, people don't do what they say they'll do because they haven't set up a way to remind themselves later.

To follow through it's important that you schedule time on your calendar to review the things that you've recorded.

Calendar

A calendar is the basic starting point with visual cues. Make sure you use one and only one calendar. Whether it's electronic or paper, know where it is and look at it regularly. Ideally you want to refer to it first thing in the morning, as needed during the day, and at the end of the day.

Be proactive, decide what you're going to do ahead of time, and schedule events and tasks. Strike a balance, though; build in enough time, be flexible with your schedule, and update it regularly.

Note: Most people over-schedule themselves.
The remedy is to identify the *essential* events and tasks, do them, and then identify minor tasks to accomplish once those are completed.

The calendar you'll use depends on your lifestyle and needs. *Ideally*, use an electronic calendar and have it synced on all your electronic devices. This allows you to keep everything up-to-date when you're out and about. *Ideally*, schedule events, tasks, and record ideas immediately. Then you can locate, refer to, and change them when you return to your office, home or hotel.

In summary:
Use your calendar regularly.
Refer to it on a regular basis.
Record things when you think of them.
Remember to update things as they change.

Schedule information on your calendar that reminds you which projects and tasks to work on, and when. In Chapter 12 I'll give more specific information on how to create and use visual cues, the best placement for your projects and tasks, the materials you'll need, and more.

Just a Simple Sticky Note

"Check this out, girl! Here's the GPS I wanted to give my cousin! Woo Hoo!"

Michelle was pleased that we'd found the long buried piece of technology under some papers in her office. "Why don't you put that in a bag near the door so you remember and take it to your car?" I suggested.

"That's a good idea. Oh man, I've got a book somebody lent me out there. I keep forgetting to bring it in," she replied. "Why not put a sticky note on the bag so when you take it out, it will remind you to bring the book in?" I offered.

Michelle looked at me in amazement and said in a really sincere tone, "Wow... that's a really high level of organizing. It would never occur to me to do that."

Sometimes just the simple humble sticky note is the key to staying organized.

Simplicity is the ultimate form of sophistication.
~ Leonardo da Vinci

Chapter 11

If Step Five is Challenging

Great things are not accomplished by those
who yield to trends and fads and popular opinion.
~ Jack Kerouac

Growing up during the 1960s and '70s I had a lot of wonderful role models who taught me to question the norm and think for myself. When I work with clients, I often notice (written kindly and without judgment) that they try to create a system of organization that's based on what someone thinks they should do rather than thinking outside the box and just doing what works for them. Or sometimes people have inherited a system that doesn't work for them but are afraid, for a variety of reasons, to redevelop it into a system that would serve them.

If Step Five is challenging perhaps it's because...

You have Multiple Calendars

These days it's easy to sync electronic calendars. You're asking for problems rather than creating solutions by using multiple calendars (or multiple other repositories where you store information that you need to remember and carry out in a timely way). Remember Step One and *simplify.* Create and use no more than you need.

You Forget to Look at Your Calendar

Some folks need to schedule the times they'll consult their calendar, others function in a more organic way and remember to consult their calendar without being reminded. If you notice you're forgetting to look at your calendar, the solution is to *create a visual cue somewhere to remind yourself.* The same goes for your tickler file (if you use one) and to-do lists for projects and tasks (we'll cover these in the next chapter).

You Forget to Record Things Immediately

Practice recording things immediately or as soon as possible, so that you don't forget. Remember, don't try to store information in your head, thinking "I'll do it in a minute," or worse, "I'll remember later." This may create stress, cause mistakes, or inhibit follow through.

The things that are easy to do are also easy not to do.
~ Jim Rohn

You're Bothered by Visual Clutter

Some people are bothered by visual clutter. If you're bothered and don't want to leave visual cues for yourself, make sure and write the reminder to carry out the task or activity somewhere you'll see it, where it *doesn't cause* visual clutter. And position it where it doesn't *get lost* in any visual clutter.

Again, you need to look to yourself and your internal process to create what's best. This is very personal and individual. Only you can devise a way to connect the dots for yourself.

You Aren't Positioning Things

If you're *not* bothered by visual cues, it may be that you aren't positioning things where they'll remind you *what* you need to do *when* you need to do it. Pay attention to how you move through time and space, and see where things are slipping through the cracks and why. Sometimes just being aware and adjusting is enough. Other times you may need to really pay attention and accept the dynamics operating in your life:

Notice, acknowledge, observe and adjust.
~ Joyce B. Wilde

Ask Yourself:

- Do I have more than one calendar?
- If yes: Why? Can I consolidate?
- Why am I not consulting my calendar?
- Why aren't visual cues working for me?
- What could I do differently to set up more effective prompts?

You're Not Moving at the Speed of Life

If you're moving too fast and attempting to do too much, it's likely that no amount of cues will suffice to keep you organized. There is a natural speed to life. Move faster than that, and life tends to find a way to slow you down -- with an illness or accident. If this is happening to you, be careful. Life may be giving you clues to slow down.

You're Not Setting Good Boundaries

The other possibility is that you're taking on too many activities and that's why you're having trouble getting and staying organized. If you've taken on too much and are trying to please too many people, you can become forgetful, cranky, and over time, ruin your health. For tips on how to set boundaries, please refer to Chapter 18.

As a wise acquaintance once said, "The definition of a boundary is where I stop and you start: physically, mentally, and emotionally." And as Bill Cosby said:

I don't know the key to success,
but the key to failure is trying to please everyone.

You're Multi-tasking

It may be that by multi-tasking you're forgetting things or mixing them up. Again, try practicing mindfulness. Place as much of your awareness on doing one thing at a time. You'll probably end up saving time, because you won't need to redo tasks, or waste time fixing things. And you won't have to revisit events or items that were forgotten or weren't done right the first time.

Subtle Self-Sabotage

To repeat what I mentioned in the beginning of this chapter, with a little bit of a different twist: it may be that you're trying to do what you *think you should do* versus what your soul is wanting you to do. I encourage you to break the rules, listen to your intuition, and do what supports you the best, instead of what you think you *have to do*.

If you don't really want to be organized (or successful, or try new things), on some level you'll sabotage yourself. If you sense this is happening, refer to the self-talk information in Chapter 17. That chapter may be especially helpful in dispelling negative thoughts that sabotage you.

Ask Yourself:
- Have I taken on too many activities and commitments?
- If so, why?
- Do I have good boundaries?
- Is multi-tasking causing things to slip through the cracks?
- Am I sabotaging myself?

Summary

Remember, these five steps are about developing new lifestyle habits, taking responsibility, seeing where you can improve, and figuring out strategies that support you and conspire to help you to be successful. If you're making some progress, but still feeling challenged in some areas, hang in there! It takes several weeks to several months to change habits.

The highest reward for man's toil is not what he gets for it,
but what he becomes by it.
~ John Ruskin

Chapter 12

Your Office

We are what we repeatedly do.
Excellence, then, is not an act, but a habit.
~ Aristotle

More and more people are establishing home offices. The advent of computers for home use is part of the reason. The retirement of baby boomers is another reason. And because of the economy, a number of home-based businesses have sprung up in recent years.

Whether you've got an office at home or at work (or both), you need to have it organized to function most effectively. Here's how:

Categories

With regard to all items in your office, let go of what you don't need (Step One). Then put everything into categories (Step Two), working from general to specific (Step Three). Establish an electronic filing system for your emails and electronic files, and a physical box, basket, tray, or bin for an:

Inbox - Items that come into your office (for example, hard copy mail).
Outbox - Items that need to leave your office.
"Things to Read" Box - Items you intend to read when you have the time.
"Things to Do" Box - Items you plan to do something with; there's some associated task.

"Missing Parts" Box - Items you need to find other parts of. (It's frustrating to find a piece of something and know you had the other piece not long ago, but you don't know where it is now!)

Also, create a box, basket, tray, or bin for items you have large quantities of, such as extra electrical cords. The problem with *not* creating a dedicated place for your various items, is that you'll have to think about them twice -- once when you get them, and then again when you're looking for them. This repetition wastes your brain power and time.

How many hours have I spent looking for things I needed?
I shudder to think of how that time could have been better spent.
~ Hana Haatainen Caye

And when you create one dedicated place for your various items -- and define them as a category -- then when you come upon other items, you can rest assured you'll know where to put them.

Visual Cues

Put the Inbox and Outbox in places that serve as visual cues. It's important to process the Inbox items on a regular basis; and it's a good idea to take the Outbox items wherever they need to go. Or put a block of time on your calendar so you remember to process them. For example, schedule time to read, or work on the items in the "Things to Do" or "Missing Parts" boxes.

As you establish these, be sure and place them in a user-friendly way. If this placement works; that's great. If not, reposition them.

If you're bothered by visual clutter, place them in a concealed area. But make sure you put a note on your calendar to remember to return to them.

Excellence is doing ordinary things extraordinarily well.
~ John W. Gardner

Projects

Here's how to organize your projects. Using the analogy of cooking on a stove, establish a physical box, basket, tray, or bin for:

Hot Projects - These are the ones that are active, on the "front burner" of your mind. They are the most important and pressing: those you are currently actively working on.

Warm Projects - These are the ones that are not as vital -- they're on the "back burner" -- but still important. You're letting them simmer for a while.

Cold Projects - These are the ones you *might* get to one day -- your "someday maybe" projects. They aren't even on the stove; you've set them off to the side, for now.

Dead Projects - These are old projects. You don't plan to do anything with them. Recycle, shred, or throw them away, if you can. If you cannot let them go, file using Archives (please refer to page 79).

It took a month to get to it and 15 minutes to remedy it.
~ Michael Greene

Positioning and Scheduling

Hopefully this seems obvious by now, however, as you establish places for your projects, position Hot Projects closest. Put Warm Projects a little further away. Cold Projects ought to be the furthest in proximity. And Dead Projects should be completely out of the way.

As you establish each place, be sure and put them in the most user-friendly way that also serves as a visual cue. And as your projects change and you have different priorities, take a moment to reposition them.

Once you establish these, and gather your items into them, then schedule a block of time on your calendar so you remember to prioritize and work on them.

The quality of a person's life is in direct proportion
to their commitment to excellence.
~ Vince Lombardi

Files

Try not to keep files on information that you can find online. With those items that remain, here's how to organize them. Establish a cabinet for:

General Reference File - Put items in which you have a small amount of information on various topics, such as: business, travel, health, investing, and so forth. If you'll use it fairly often, put it where you can easily access it.

Topic Specific Reference File - Put items in which you have a large amount of specific information on one topic, such as if you travel extensively, or collect a lot of information about health. This file is used when you want to create one broad category with a lot of subcategories.

Again, if you'll use it often, put it where you can easily access it, if not, put it out of the way.

Archives - Put items that are no longer active, like back taxes, or other "dead" files. These are the files you need to keep but don't want taking up space in your "Prime Real Estate." Position these *well* out of the way, in a storage area or basement; but, make sure it's accessible.

Tickler File - This is a physical structure that contains hanging file folders. These folders have the days of the month and months of the year. This file allows you to put items in repositories so you remember to carry out tasks or projects at certain times. It works for some people but not for others. It's obvious but needs to be mentioned: *It only works if you use it.* Make sure it is easily accessible.

For each file, establish a box, basket, tray, or bin -- a "holding station" -- where items will go until they are filed (unless of course, you or someone else always files things immediately).

To-Do Lists

When you create to-do notes for projects and tasks, it's okay to mix them if they are related. For example, tasks that need completed in a day are considered one category ("Saturday's tasks"). Whereas tasks for different projects should not be mixed -- unless you have a way to sort and prioritize them. Generally it's best to use separate electronic documents, or separate pieces of paper.

Again, the keys to being successful are recording items when they occur to you and referring to them regularly. Also, update things as they change, and check them off, but don't delete them when they're finished. You may need to refer back to them at some point.

The key is not to prioritize what's on your schedule,
but to schedule your priorities.
~ Stephen Covey

Office Materials

It's important to have office materials available, and ones that are frequently used, positioned nearby. Organizing becomes aggravating if you don't have the simple things on hand and accessible, like: hanging file folders, manila folders, labels, markers, sticky notes, paper clips, stapler and staples, for example. Isn't it a drag to run out of staples and not have more when you need them? Make a list of what you need and schedule a time when those items will be replenished.

It's important to have the materials to create the labels readily available. If the materials aren't available, people often fail to create them.

In reading over the lives of great men,
I found that the first victory they won was over themselves...
self-discipline with all of them came first.
~ Harry Truman

Labels

Labels are important visual cues. Make sure and label *everything* that's appropriate: items, projects, files, to-do lists, and so on. Always be sure and label things clearly so *they* don't get mixed up, and *you* don't get mixed up.

Sometimes people are too eager to begin labeling. Label things temporarily, until you're sure they'll work for you. Use the areas, and temporary labels, for a little while; then label them permanently, if needed. And if things are self-evident, perhaps no labels are necessary.

You are not here merely to make a living.
You are here in order to enable the world to live more amply,
with greater vision,
with a finer spirit of hope and achievement.
You are here to enrich the world,
and you impoverish yourself if you forget the errand.
~ Woodrow Wilson

Chapter 13

Putting All Five Steps Together

Beethoven was deaf, Milton was blind,
but their names will last as long as time endures, because they dreamed
and translated their dreams into organized thought.

~ Napoleon Hill

"It's impossible, Joyce. Ever since I retired, I just can't seem to get my act together. What ideas do you have?" Ken asked.

Ken is highly creative, yet he was used to being creative *within* the confines of an eight-to-five schedule. In the past six months, he had gotten his fill of staying up all hours of the night and sleeping until noon. He enjoyed hanging out with family and friends and being non-productive. He was having fun, but it was coming at an expense. His house was getting cluttered, his health was suffering, and he wasn't keeping up with his paperwork or paying bills.

I asked him three questions: *If you could wave a magic wand, what would you create in your life? Why? How?*

In answer to the *What* question, Ken said, "I want to organize my home, office, and time." In answer to *Why?* He answered, "To enjoy a balanced 'body, mind, spirit' approach to life." In answer to *How?* He said, "I want to use your five steps."

Body, Mind, Spirit

Here is how we used my five steps:

Step One - I helped Ken **let go** of all unnecessary items in every room of his home, including his home office. We reviewed how he was spending his time, and we identified one primary drain: Internet surfing. He agreed to cut down the amount of time he was spending on the Internet and limit his use to an hour a day. Although this wasn't easy, he could see that by letting go, he could gain.

Step Two - We **categorized** all of his belongings and his paperwork. We created a schedule by categorizing his day into three parts. To support his body, he spent mornings either at the gym or walking with a friend. To support his mind, he spent afternoons managing his home, processing his paperwork, and reading. In the late afternoon, he would reward himself with an hour on the Internet. To support his "spirit," he spent evenings doing various activities with family and friends. This daily balance suited him.

Step Three - We worked from **general to specific** by identifying what needed organized first. We created a plan of action that began with a general decluttering. Then we addressed some more specific projects that included his paperwork and making his kitchen more user-friendly and functional. Ken found it helpful to start organizing his time in a general sense, and eventually he began to incorporate some more specific activities. He began to fish, garden and cook.

Step Four - We **placed closest** to him what he'd use often. We identified the best places for him to keep his gym equipment, and then his fishing and gardening supplies. We also changed his kitchen around a couple different times as he discovered what worked best for him.

Step Five - We created **visual cues** by scheduling his daily list of activities and events on his calendar. And we used other visual prompts to remind him what needed done with his paperwork. He used an **audio cue** to remind him to stop Internet surfing after one hour.

I worked with him once a week for a period of time. We began our sessions by celebrating his progress, and we reviewed his challenges. In a matter of weeks, he was on his way to being back in balance and happily retired.

The glory of human nature lies in our seeming capacity
to exercise conscious control of our own destiny.
~ Winston Churchill

Hard Copy Mail

Here's how to stay organized using these five steps with hard copy mail:

Step One - When the mail comes in *if you have the time*, immediately recycle or shred what isn't needed (**let go**). If you're motivated, **reduce the flow in** by registering online, or use the app of your preference.

Step Two - When the mail comes in, if you *don't* have the time to process it immediately, scan for anything really important and **categorize** by putting it in your Hot Projects. Divide the rest of the mail into your Inbox or your Things to Read box. Another common category people create is for shopping/coupons.

Step Three - You've already done this step (worked from **general to specific**), when you set out what's important (putting items into Hot Projects); and what's not immediately important (putting items into your Inbox and Things to Read box).

Step Four - Make sure your Hot Projects tray is **positioned nearby**, so it's convenient to process your important mail.

Step Five - Make sure you've positioned your Inbox where you see it, so you'll have a **visual cue** to return to it and process the items when you have time. If it's important to return to the Things to Read box, put a **note on your calendar** to do so.

Action expresses priorities.
~ Mahatma Gandhi

Ideas that Inspire You

Here's an example of how Al, a copy editor and writer, uses my five steps to organize ideas for his books, articles, and film scripts. Like many middle-aged individuals, he uses a combination of paper and electronic formats to capture his ideas.

Step One - Al is extremely creative, has many great ideas, and is learning to ask himself if the idea is *really* something he'll want to develop. If not, he's learning to **let go**. In doing so, he's more able to focus on what he really enjoys.

Steps Two and Three - Often his ideas come when he's not near a computer, so he uses a combination of his smart phone and small paper notebooks, which he keeps in his briefcase and car.

He was having problems categorizing his ideas and we identified that the difficulty was due to mixing notes. He would put ideas for two or three different articles in one electronic document or on one piece of paper. And they weren't clearly labeled.

Now he **categorizes** working from **general to specific**. He asks himself: Is this for a book, article, or film script? When I think of this project, what's the first thing that comes to mind? Do I need to create a new folder or is there an existing one I could add to? Do I need to create a new document or is there one with related ideas? Should the labels include dates as well as titles? Do I need to change the number of the draft?

Step Four - Al keeps the projects for which he has the most passion and enthusiasm **closest at hand.** And he gets the ones that are finished out of the way.

Step Five - He uses his electronic devices to create visual cues. He **schedules time** to work on his various current projects, and also future related events.

Great things are done by a series of small things put together.
~ Vincent Van Gogh

Yarn, Thread, and "This 'n' That"

Bonnie, a retired Home Economics teacher, was overwhelmed at the prospect of downsizing the extensive array of items in her sewing room. Here is how we used my five steps:

Step One - I said to her, "If it's not going to live here anymore it needs to leave here. Let's **let go** of things you know for sure you won't be using again." We sorted through her items and she identified lots of supplies she won't use again.

Step Two - Then I said, "Let's put things in **categories**." Because she needed to *drastically* downsize and split up her items, putting many into storage, I suggested the categories would be "sooner" and "later." And the subcategories were yarn, thread, glue, etc.

After we subcategorized the items we put them in boxes. Then we labeled them. Next we stored them where she knew she'd look for them next time. (Note: Depending on your personality and needs, you may wish to also create inventory forms that list all of the items, and file the forms.)

Step Three - We worked from **general to specific.** In this case that was the process of letting go, dividing items into "sooner" versus "later," then dividing into subcategories, labeling them, and then storing the boxes.

Step Four - As we worked, we **kept closest** what she used most often. We put the items she'll use "sooner" in an area that's easier for her to access (in this case, her den). And we placed the items she'll use "later" further away (in this case, a storage area).

Step Five - We created and used **visual cues** by scheduling blocks of time on her calendar to remind her to return to the "sooner" projects and work on them.

> *Hide not your talents, they for use were made,*
> *What's a sundial in the shade?*
> ~ Ben Franklin

Photos

Jim is a charming elderly widower who has many thousands of photos that date back to early last century. He travels extensively, and most of the photos were from trips he'd taken. He wasn't interested in scanning them into his computer. He was content with organizing them in hard copy. Here's how we used my steps:

Step One - Jim decided he didn't want to review his negatives so we **let them go**. We threw them and their plastic jackets away and we recycled the heavy paper envelopes in which they were contained.

Step Two - He identified a time period, year, or a trip with the date (e.g., "1950s" or "1990" or "Morocco/1996"). Next we **created a category** for each. We used boxes and bags, and labeled them temporarily by using sticky notes.

Note: Remember, do what works for you.
One of Jim's categories was "I can't remember" and another was
"I want to slowly peruse these and think about where I want them."

Step Three - We worked from **general to specific** by creating the repositories (boxes and bags) as a starting point. We returned to each specific category (decade, year, or trip) and processed and organized it more at a later date.

Step Four - We put the items Jim wanted to revisit soon in a handy location. We **kept them closest** by placing them in the front of his office cabinet. We put the photos he had less interest in looking at again in his spare bedroom.

Step Five - We **scheduled times on his calendar** for us to continue working on the project together, and for him to work on it alone. And we also identified and scheduled times for him to share the photos with friends and family.

We make a living by what we get, we make a life by what we give.
~ Winston Churchill

You May Not Use All Five Steps Every Time

Here's an excerpt from an email of a teacher who used my steps successfully:

"I created four dozen packets of information for the students and only used about half of them. Normally I have to make packets each time because I'm not very organized. This time, because of our work together, it occurred to me to do Step Two and create a category for the ones that remained.

I got a box, labeled it clearly, and neatly put the remainder inside. Then I did Step Four by placing the box in a closet near where I'll need it. And I carried out Step Five by putting a note to remind me next time. I'm so pleased!"

Man's mind, stretched by a new idea,
never goes back to its original dimensions.
~ Oliver Wendell Holmes, Jr.

Chapter 14

To Stay Organized: Change Lifestyle Habits

In the realm of ideas, everything depends on enthusiasm;
in the real world, all rests on perseverance.
~ Johann Wolfgang von Goethe

One of my neighbors learned that I'm a professional organizer and looked in my car to see if it was organized. I thought that was brilliant. Richard wanted to see if I walk my talk.

Yes, I do.

And I do it in a balanced way. My car is *fairly* organized *most* of the time, but not *always* organized *all* of the time. I'm not interested in being perfectly organized, and you shouldn't be either. I'm interested in using my time and doing my tasks efficiently. I pay attention to the flow of what needs to be done, when it needs to be done, and how it can be done in the most effective manner. That's the goal.

And by doing that, I have achieved, over time, a high level of organization in a variety of settings. And that's why I started my organizing/coaching business and wrote this book -- to help others do so, too.

Entropy

Entropy is defined as, "A gradual decline into disorder." It's a normal thing. It's one of the laws of nature. Look at what happens to your garden or lawn. Grass grows and weeds appear. Plants need to be watered and tomatoes need to be staked. Unless you trim and weed, you are one good rain away from a jungle.

Things tend to fall into disarray and disrepair not because something is wrong; but just because that's the nature of life. Everything can't immediately be attended to. Work, plans, kids and family get in the way.

The "Wave" and Three Ways to Approach it

As I mentioned in Chapter 7, there's a natural flow to life. Things tend to happen in waves. The trick is to get to things as you can -- before the waves rise too high and you suffer a tsunami.

For example, most of us cannot file or put things away immediately. The remedy is what I mentioned in Step Two: establish physical boxes, baskets, trays, or bins where you put items that you (or someone else) will file or put away when there's time. Then schedule a time for this to be done.

Or just do it in an organic way -- when you see things are building up, or they are getting on your nerves; then do them. But *don't* put them off indefinitely.

Listen to the natural rhythm and flow of life and respond to it. There are several ways to make this part of your lifestyle habits:

Approach #1 - Dedicate a longer block of time to process and organize.

If things have really built up, estimate how long it will take to complete the task and schedule a block of time (Step Five) to address it. This period of time may range from an hour, to a day, or multiple sessions over time.

Approach #2 - Organize in the "nooks and crannies" by dedicating a smaller amount of time.

Do the tasks quickly if you are willing to interrupt what you're doing to carry them out and they can be done in a relatively short amount of time (10 to 20 minutes, or so).

Approach #3 - Do the task immediately.

Do the task if it can be done very quickly at the moment you're thinking of it -- if it doesn't interrupt the flow of your work or your thought processes.

Example

In the case of filing, if you've let it build up for many weeks, months or years, you would probably want to use the first approach. If you have let the filing build up for a short time, you may be able to catch up on it in a short time and would use the second approach. An example of the third choice would be filing a paper right in the moment it needs to be done.

Either way, there's an investment in time. And either you'll spend some time on the front end organizing yourself, or you'll waste time (energy and money) on the back end trying to find things, paying late fees, etc.

My favorite things in life don't cost any money.
It's really clear that the most precious resource we all have is time.
~ Steve Jobs

Your Energy

It's important to pay attention to your energy, and to the extent you have the flexibility, do your letting go and categorizing at times that are compatible with the level and strength of your energy. You can also learn how to shift your energy, especially when you're feeling blocked on certain tasks. See Chapter 16 for more information on this subject.

Honoring your energy is an important part of making these your lifestyle habits. Find ways to do these tasks so they bring you energy rather than leave you depleted. Equate this to exercise; the best way to stay in shape is by picking exercise you enjoy, and doing it at a time when you have the best energy.

He who lives in harmony with himself
lives in harmony with the universe.
~ Marcus Aurelius

Boundaries and Communication

As you begin to implement these five habits, and review your time and tasks, you may realize you're involved in too many activities. If you're serious about changing your lifestyle habits, you may need to set boundaries and let go of some of the volunteer work and other commitments you have *that no longer suit you.* Give yourself permission. This is a form of letting go.

Recently I was working with a client who is starting her own home-based business. She needed to process and organize her belongings before welcoming clients into her home. We decided she would spend two hours each day working toward her goal of creating a business. Eventually she'll stop working for her employer.

She's a busy married mother of three: works, drives her kids to their activities, and makes meals. Someone at her job asked if she'd participate in a volunteer activity. It sounded like fun, and was a tough decision. She knew if she accepted, she wouldn't be able to keep the commitment she made to spend time each day creating the business she's passionate about.

She thought it through and decided to say no to the volunteer activity. She used some of the communication techniques you'll learn in Chapter 18. Set healthy boundaries, and learn to communicate them. Create a lifestyle to support your dreams.

Half of the troubles of this life can be traced to saying yes too quickly and not saying no soon enough.

~ Josh Billings

Chapter 15

Disorganized: Intention and Action Don't Match

You cannot prevent the birds of sorrow from flying over your head,
but you can prevent them from building nests in your hair.
~ Chinese Proverb

Do you say things like:

- *I like to talk about getting organized and always hope I will, but I never do.* - or -
- *I have a bunch of books about organizing. I love to read them, but for some reason I'm* still *not organized.* - or -
- *It feels like when I start organizing, things get worse rather than better.* - or -
- *I want it done perfectly,* now, *and I never end up getting any of it done, or just part of it and it's not very satisfying.* - or -
- *I invite a friend over to help me organize but then we end up talking and I can tell I'm delaying. Finally my friend* makes *me organize.*

If you relate to any of the statements above, or if you sense some subtle -- or not so subtle -- sabotage in your efforts to get and stay organized, perhaps you need to apply actions that are in alignment with your intentions.

Talk doesn't cook rice.
~ Chinese Proverb

Ask Yourself:

- Am I frustrated because what I say I'll do and what I actually do don't match up?
- Why don't my intentions and actions match?
- How might I change these dynamics?
- Am I empowered to make changes in the situation I'm in?
- If yes: How? And if not: Why not?

Do any of these situations resonate with you? Write or talk a little more about what you experience.

Sabotage

Have you ever smoked cigarettes? I did. And I learned by trial and error that after I quit, if I got into a romantic relationship with a man who smoked, it wouldn't be long before I would be "bumming a smoke" -- and not long after that I'd be back to a regular habit of smoking daily. At first I didn't know that would be the outcome, but once I knew that, and continued to do it, I was sabotaging my efforts not to smoke.

It's a good example of sabotage, or not aligning intention and action.

Another example of sabotage is when you quit smoking and someone -- who knows you quit smoking -- gives you a carton of your favorite brand of cigarettes shortly after you quit. Be careful of people's influence on you.

You Have Choices

When you want to change something in your life, you have four choices:

1. Change the situation.
2. Change your view of the situation.
3. Change your behaviors to match or complement the situation.
4. Leave the situation.

Success is more accurately measured by the obstacles overcome,
than by the position one has reached.
~ Booker T. Washington

Choice #1

As organizing is concerned, in order to change the situation:

A. Learn the Five Steps I have presented.
B. Carry them out on a regular basis.
C. Practice mindfulness: Stay present. Then notice and adjust as necessary.

You become aware of things you might change by your own discovery or someone else's input. Then you change habits by your willingness and follow through.

Choice #2

You can change your view of the situation by understanding that what bothers one person doesn't necessarily bother another. For example, visual clutter may greatly bother you, whereas your partner may block it out and truly isn't bothered.

I have made a ceaseless effort not to ridicule, not to bewail,
not to scorn human actions, but to understand them.
~ Baruch Spinoza

Choice #3

"I tell kids, 'If you know your parents are going to tell you to take the trash out, be smart. Do it before they ask,'" Sergeant Tim Lumas told me. The good sergeant worked actively with children and teenagers. I thought his advice was incredibly insightful. It was about being proactive.

Behavior is what a man does, not what he thinks, feels, or believes.
~ Emily Dickinson

Being proactive means to think and act ahead of anticipated events. It can be a powerful strategy. But sometimes there's joy in resisting. If you're having fun resisting something, and want to be proactive to change it, you need to become aware of what you're doing and consciously choose to make new choices.

Choice #4

After you exercise the first three choices, the last choice is to leave a situation you cannot change, and can no longer tolerate. However, the reason I'm writing about these choices is that people often become upset and leap to choice number four before fully exploring their other options.

When you discover that you are riding a dead horse,
the best strategy is to dismount.
~ Dakota Tribal Saying

Leaving may be the best choice, or it may reflect all-or-nothing thinking. This happens when people become frustrated and reach their limit ("It's my way or the highway.")

Be careful about making this last choice, as "black and white" thinking doesn't help when you're trying to develop new choices and solve problems. It's very helpful to learn to operate in the grey area and remember that, as organizing is concerned, it's a process, not an all-or-nothing event.

Ask Yourself:

- Am I approaching getting and staying organized as a choice rather than a "have to" or a "should?"
- Am I dealing adequately with the emotions of grief, guilt, shame, and pleasure?
- What's stopping me from setting boundaries and limiting the flow in?
- What's keeping me from saying *no* and limiting my tasks and activities?
- Is there some way to view the challenges I'm experiencing as opportunities for growth and change?

Choices Summarized

Make it a choice to get and stay organized. Don't force yourself to deal with the stuff in your office, home, or head. If you do, your mind may resent your efforts and keep you disorganized.

If memories of grief, guilt, or shame are getting triggered, the most empowering way to handle them is to *want to* deal with them, not *have to* (for whatever reasons). Usually *have to* and *should* are emotionally heavy and rob you of the energy needed to sort things out. Try to become aware and turn *have to* into *want to* and *should* into *choose to* so you don't create an emotional state that depletes and weakens you. Read on for more ideas of ways to get in touch with these thoughts and change them.

All men should strive to learn before they die;
what they are running from, and to, and why.
~ James Thurber

Chapter 16

The Psychology of Energy

Energy medicine is the future of all medicine.

~ Dr. Oz

Recently I was working with Joanie, and after about twenty minutes she began to lose energy. It was as if she was a plant that needed water. I asked her what she was thinking. She thought about it for a moment and said, "I can't make decisions." I thanked her for honestly sharing what she was thinking and replied, "I'm puzzled, though, because I've watched you make decisions for the past twenty minutes."

She responded, "Okay... it's more accurate to say, I have a *hard time* making decisions, so this is hard, and I'm feeling a lot of resistance to continuing." I said, "It's great you can hear what you're thinking. It's what's called a 'core negative message' or 'limiting core belief.' It's a thought that makes it hard to carry out positive actions that support your goals." Then I asked if she'd be open to doing some energy medicine techniques. She was. We did them together and in a matter of minutes she returned to the process of letting go and creating categories, and we worked together with no problem for the remainder of the afternoon.

I'll talk more about limiting core beliefs and how to change them in the next chapter. For now, I'll continue on the topic of energy medicine.

Age, Energy, and Organizing

When you're younger, you can "muscle through" a lot of barriers. As time goes on, this can become more challenging. Alternative medicine is one avenue to support and strengthen energy.

For other individuals, no matter what age, just the *thought* of organizing lessens their energy. Or you may find that when you actually *begin* to organize and come upon memorabilia that triggers uncomfortable memories and feelings, you feel resistant to carrying out necessary tasks. Again, alternative medicine approaches can be helpful for moving past those blocks and shifting the discomfort.

New opinions are always suspected, and usually opposed,
without any other reason but because they are not already common.
~ John Locke

A Return to Health

The winter of 2010 I quit drinking coffee and black tea. I'd had a 30-year habit of using those substances, so this was no small order.

A massage therapist gave me Donna Eden's *Energy Medicine* book. I began doing Donna's Five-Minute Energy Medicine Routine on a daily basis, in the morning, to energize myself.

It's not a jolt like caffeine, however I found it helped lift, clear and balance my energy. And I noticed that I began approaching and experiencing life with less resistance. I began to share it with my family, friends, and clients.

Energy medicine resonates with me on a common sense level, because forms of it were used centuries ago in Chinese Medicine. For me, energy medicine also resonates on a common sense level because the body is made up of energy. Energy is stored in the body, and thoughts and words have energy. Read the book *Power vs. Force* by Dr. David R. Hawkins, M.D. PhD., to learn more about the science that supports kinesiology, or muscle-testing, which is an integral aspect of energy medicine.

Why do I feel so strongly about this? I got sick and almost died during the winter of 2010. I was diagnosed with Interstitial Cystitis and told there was no cure. The doctors gave me five rounds of antibiotics. I became bedridden, and could barely function. The pain was excruciating. Then they prescribed pain medications, but I refused.

As I mention in my biography, I am a long-time recovering alcoholic. I knew that taking pain medications could trigger a relapse and I wasn't willing to risk it. Also, I had the audacity (as the doctors saw it) to ask *why* I was in pain, and stated that I wanted to be *healed*, not *treated*.

Out of desperation, I turned to my mother, who is fit and fabulous -- and in her late 70s. She connected me with doctors who practice a combination of "East-meets-West" medicine. I was accurately diagnosed with Adrenal Fatigue and have since fully recovered. As a result of my experiences, I began to open my mind to new ways of seeing things.

No problem can be solved
from the same level of consciousness that created it.
~ Albert Einstein

Paradigm Shift

This chapter was tough for me to write; I feel like I'm "coming out of the closet" as a Master's level psychologist. Philosophically this is a huge paradigm shift from the education and training I received in Clinical Psychology.

I was taught to see what's wrong with people (pathology-based thinking), quantify symptoms as disorders, and use labels to define them. Then the solution was to apply medicine.

I realized there was something wrong with me...
and it is that I think there is something wrong with me.
~ Jon Swift

Using labels and medicines *can* have great value, and are useful for communicating (and necessary in many systems for billing and reimbursement). This approach can also be limiting, even damaging. Very often, only the symptoms are treated; the roots of the illnesses are not addressed.

Western (allopathic) Medicine was designed to be used in crisis situations. It was not originally intended for ongoing palliative care. From a strictly Western perspective there is often not much discussion of a positive, strength-based approach (by "strength-based" I mean one that emphasizes strengths and interests, including creativity and spirituality). And usually no alternative "woo-woo" stuff is considered, because much of it hasn't yet been validated by science.

Often in the real world, experience precedes science. I have learned there are growing numbers of people trying alternative methods of health care, including Dr. Christiane Northrup, Deepak Chopra, Dr. Lewis Mehl-Madrona, and Caroline Myss.

Reexamine all you have been told... dismiss what insults your soul.
~ Walt Whitman

The Way of the Future

Chiropractors were considered quacks when I was growing up. Over the past thirty or forty years, that field has become legitimate and accepted. I believe it will be the same with energy medicine, and other alternative approaches to health.

A recent survey by HealthFocus International found that 45% of adults were concerned about feeling tired. In fact, fatigue is the fourth most common health complaint, affecting 28.5 million Americans -- and it's a growing concern.

Marcelle Pick RNC, MSN, OB/GYN, NP, author of *Are You Tired or Wired?* estimates that 80% of Americans are suffering from Adrenal Fatigue. James L. Wilson, ND, DC, PhD, author of *Adrenal Fatigue* estimates that number to be at least 60%. And the experts at the Centers for Disease Control and Prevention say that between one and four million Americans are affected by a debilitating condition called Chronic Fatigue Syndrome.

Increasing caffeine intake may cause a case of the jitters, so as a result, more and more individuals are turning to alternative methods to increase their energy. It can also be useful in shifting the blocks you feel to doing certain tasks. Organizing is one of those experiences that tend to create, or expose, resistance.

It's About the Intention

Some people are put off by the thought of alternative medicine because they view it as New Age and in conflict with their religious beliefs. The dictionary definition of New Age is "thought that began in about the last half of last century."

If we didn't use anything that was thought of since then, we wouldn't be using an awful lot of things, including a computer or cell phone. There have -- and always will be -- new ideas and inventions. I view them simply as tools.

Much of alternative medicine works on the level of the *power of intention.* For me, the intention behind something is what's important. A kitchen knife can be used to make a meal, or to hurt somebody. What matters is our intentions and how we choose to use tools.

Make sure your motivation is right
or you won't get good results.

~ Anonymous

Alternative medicine is very similar to prayer, which is about sending positive intentions. For me, since alternative medicine is similar, it can be allied with -- rather than in conflict with -- religious or spiritual beliefs.

Organizing and Energy

Try using Donna Eden's Five-Minute Routine (you can locate it with a quick Internet search) before you begin to organize, or when you begin to feel blocked while organizing. Pay attention to your energy and use the techniques that resonate with you when you feel your energy decreasing. When I'm working with people I sometimes feel their energy decrease and I encourage them to use energy medicine alone, or in combination with talking.

Talking is a good starting point; it can be very helpful in identifying underlying challenges and triggers. I call it "naming the monster" or "giving voice to the experience," and this is important. However, sometimes talking may arouse internal demons that keep you stuck in the story. You'll sense that you're stuck when you keep repeating yourself and the result is you feel agitated or drained of energy. The solution is to stay in the moment and pay attention to the flow of energy, and adjust as needed.

Circumventing the story via natural means can be powerful. If you're talking about your problems, and organizing challenges, and finding it draining, try Donna Eden's Five-Minute Routine, then *take constructive action.*

It's Inexpensive and Readily Available

One thing that's appealing about energy medicine is that it's free (or inexpensive). And again, an Internet search will quickly get you started. You can find the Five-Minute Routine on YouTube. And if you want other inexpensive resources, try Donna Eden's Energy Medicine Kit.

If you don't feel drawn to Donna's approach, you may wish to try some other forms of alternative medicine such as EFT (Emotional Freedom Technique), Essential Oils, Homeopathy, Chinese Energy Medicine, Energetic Well Being, Access Bars, and Jo Dunning's Pulse Technique.

There are probably lots more; these are just some that people have shared with me. Meditation and yoga are very well aligned with these forms of medicine, and I strongly recommend them. They are all complementary with Western medicine. Do some experimenting and find what works for you.

But what is happiness except the simple harmony
between a man and the life he leads?
~ Albert Camus

Make it Your Lifestyle

The ideas in this book are designed to help you learn to get and stay organized by converting these five steps into habits that you incorporate into your lifestyle. Doing the Five-Minute Energy Medicine Routine on a daily basis uses the same approach. I encourage you to make it (or other approaches that work for you) part of your daily routine. You may find that you are more in the flow, with increased energy. And hopefully, you will be able to organize your time and tasks with less effort.

Recently I was speaking to a group and someone asked about my strategy on carrying out tasks, time management and energy. She said she noticed I talk a lot about honoring your energy and working with it.

Pay attention to your energy and -- to the extent you have the flexibility -- carry out tasks that are compatible with its current strength and level. Build as much flexibility into your days as you can.

As you have read, I encourage you to notice and adjust. When you get in the habit of doing energy medicine, you'll begin to sense when your energy gets weaker. Learn to listen to your energy and support it.

Support Yourself

If you decide to use Donna's Five-Minute Energy Medicine Routine, remember my Step Four and find a handy place to keep your energy medicine information (summary of the Five-Minute Routine and/or other information). That way you support rather than sabotage your efforts.

Also, use my Step Five and establish a visual cue somewhere, so you are reminded to carry out the Five-Minute Routine on a regular basis. And establish a visual cue to remind you to use it -- or some of her other techniques -- when you feel like organizing but the thought of it kills your energy.

The man with a new idea is a crank until the new idea succeeds.
~ Mark Twain

Chapter 17

Self Talk: Don't "Should" on Yourself

It is a well-known fact that one comes, finally, to BELIEVE whatever one repeats to one's self, whether the statement be true or false.
~ Napoleon Hill

"I have *bad habits* when it comes to organizing. I should be doing this better," Anne hissed quietly at herself as she sat hunched over some paperwork in her office. "Would it be accurate to say you have frequently occurring behaviors that don't support your desire to be organized?" I gently asked.

She looked over at me, surprised, sat up straight, and replied, "Exactly! How did you know? And how do I change this?"

Anne's words *"bad habits"* and tone of voice told me she was shaming herself, so I deliberately reframed them using compassionate communication. Thinking and speaking in a negative way can drain you.

One of the most simple, yet powerful things I learned when I got my Masters degree in Clinical Psychology was the play on words, "Don't should on yourself." -- So then what *do* you do?

Modify Your Thinking

Resistance to organizing begins in the brain and usually sounds like:

I should do it... I know I should, but I can't... I need to, but I don't know where to begin... It's hopeless... I'll never be able to... I can't do it... It'll never change....

Sound familiar?

This is what I often hear when I work with people. It's called negative self-talk, and it's driven by "core negative messages." It's very challenging to get and stay organized with this going on in your head.

We will act consistently with our view of who we are,
whether that view is accurate or not.
~ Anthony Robbin

Begin to catch your negative thoughts and replace them with positive empowering ones like:

I want to do it... I know I can, somehow... I can try, and what I don't know, I'll learn... There's always hope... I am determined to find a way... I can... It will change....

Become Your Own Best Friend

How do you catch negative thoughts and replace them with positive, empowering ones? Try mindfulness. Start to pay attention to the thoughts you think:

• When you notice they are negative, until you get successful at changing them to positive ones, at least try to use more neutral words.

• If you can't hear your negative messages, start to pay attention to your thoughts *specifically when you're getting ready to do something you're afraid of, or don't want to do.* This is the time these thoughts are the most obvious (one indicator is that you feel edgy).

- If you're in a bad place, gently help yourself by practicing kindness in your thoughts and patience in your actions.

- When you say you haven't accomplished something, add "yet!" to the end of the sentence.

- Catch yourself when you're doing *really well* and reward yourself -- to positively reinforce your progress.

- When you notice your thought processes are becoming more positive, take time to celebrate in some way. At least take a moment and pat yourself on the back.

> *To change one's life, start immediately,*
> *do it flamboyantly, no exceptions.*
> ~ William James

Easier Said than Done

This is all easier said than done, right? It's because the brain has what's called "Negativity Bias." Negative thoughts stick like Velcro, but positive thoughts don't, they often flow off like Teflon. One way to get positive thoughts to stay is to focus on what you're happy about for 20 or 25 seconds.

Another analogy of how the brain works is the "Luge" event at the Winter Olympics. The luge is the small sled the racers use to go down snow-laden icy pathways.

Over time, the brain develops well-worn avenues of thought. They operate with the same fast and seemingly automatic process -- of which we're often not aware. And that's why it's so hard to change negative behaviors, because automatic negative thoughts are driving them.

By the way, don't be embarrassed by your negative thoughts, we all have them. And most people say things to themselves they would *never* say to anyone else.

> *Everyone thinks of changing the world,*
> *but no one thinks of changing himself.*
> ~ Andrew Carnegie

Ask Yourself:

- Am I aware when I tell myself I "should," or I "have to"?
- Am I aware of other negative self-talk?
- What triggers my negative thoughts?
- Am I blaming others for the way I think or behave?
- What are ways I can empower myself to change these dynamics?

The Power of Words

"They're just words!" Claire, a young redhead at a workshop recently exclaimed.

"Sticks and stones may break my bones, but words will never hurt me," is a very inaccurate statement, in my humble view. And I am not alone in that viewpoint. I attended many of Dr. Marshall Rosenberg's Compassionate Communication workshops and he agrees, and stresses the point that words are very powerful.

Words start wars. And those wars begin in our own brains, as author Eckhart Tolle puts it, between the "I" and the "me." If you're able to see this in yourself, that's a good start:

> *Healthy discontent is the prelude to progress.*
> ~ Mahatma Gandhi

Thoughts are Things

"Be careful what you're thinking. Thoughts are things," said Marc as we walked on the beach. He gave this input after listening to me puzzle over something I was feeling upset about.

I thought what he said was extremely insightful. I imagined thoughts being like clothes that I put on hangers into the closet of my brain. I can choose to fill my brain-closet with good and helpful attire, or garments that make me want to slam the doors and run away.

If you have an inclination to write, journaling regularly can help you get in touch with negative thoughts. See if you find yourself constantly writing about things that bug you.

> *When people find out what it is that's ticking in them*
> *they get straightened out.*
> ~ Joseph Campbell

Talking to a friend, family member, or professional can be a big help, too. Just make sure you don't get stuck in a negative story and keep repeating it. That can have the effect of reinforcing rather than letting it go, due to "self-fulfilling prophecies."

> *Don't name a dog "Trouble" or that's just what you might get.*
> ~ Anonymous

Ignoring negative thoughts doesn't make them go away. To change the negative messages in your head, first you need to get in touch with them. And nobody but you can do this for you.

Hear It then Change It

About now your brain may be saying, "This will never work."

If you can hear that, *good*, it's an example. You've just identified a negative thought. Write it down. Once you have a list of them, you'll create right and left brain positive counter-statements. It's another way to change the "luge" in your brain. These are like positive affirmations with feet on them. Next we'll put these positive affirmations into motion to help resolve and dissolve subtle forms of sabotage.

> *If you want things to be different,*
> *perhaps the answer is to become different yourself.*
> ~ Norman Vincent Peale

Core Negative Messages or Limiting Core Beliefs

Negative thoughts are called "core negative messages" by some, and "limiting core beliefs" by others. Whichever way you view it, they are the thoughts that get in the way of you being all that you can be. Here's how it works:

The left side of the brain is the logical part; the right side of the brain is the intuitive/artist part. The left side hears what sounds like negative statements in a positive way. For example, "fight breast cancer" is a positive left brain statement, whereas "support breast health" is a positive right brain statement.

Other examples: "hate isn't a family value" is a positive left brain statement, whereas "love is a family value" is a positive right brain statement. And "war isn't the answer" is a positive left brain statement, whereas "peace is the answer" is a positive right brain statement.

Below are examples of limiting core beliefs clients have shared with me while working on their organizing efforts. Beneath them are left and right brain "counter" statements, that take into account the different ways the brain works:

Negative message: "This will never work."
Right brain - "This *will* work."
Left brain - "This hasn't worked before, however I'm willing to give it another try."

Negative message: "I can't decide."
Right brain - "I *can* decide!"
Left brain - "I can't decide at this moment, however, momentarily it'll become clear."

Negative message: "I'll never be able to do this."
Right brain - "I *am* able to do this."
Left brain - "I haven't been able to do this, but I'll try again."

If you think you can do a thing
or think you can't do a thing, you're right.
~ Henry Ford

One way to change these core statements is to say the new left and right brain positive statements out loud while doing Donna Eden's Temporal Tap technique: Spread your fingers and tap (or rub) on your head on the areas surrounding your ears (above and behind) as you repeat the positive messages. You may wish to Google Donna Eden's Temporal Tap YouTube video for more specific information.

Ask Yourself:

- What are my core negative statements? (Some people can easily identify them, whereas for others it takes some thought and introspection.)
- How are they getting in the way of organizing?
- Am I willing to try new methods to change them?
- In what ways would I benefit by creating more positive thoughts?
- What outcome would I like to see from my efforts?

More about Core Negative Messages

Below are more examples of negative statements clients have shared with me:

"I can't remember."

"I don't know enough."

"I'll never get it done."

"I distract easily."

"I'll be wrong [on the simplest things]."

"I can't think and as a result I freeze."

Sometimes what drives these statements is the all-or-nothing thinking I mentioned earlier. Take small steps to make changes to these powerful negative messages. If you try to change everything all at once, it's like making a new year's resolution to exercise an hour a day when you haven't been exercising at all!

A journey of a thousand miles begins with a single step.

~ Lao Tzu

Empower Yourself

Now take your list of negative messages and write your positive left and right brain counter statements. Don't worry about getting too precise, or doing it perfectly, just give it a try. Remember, it's about the intention.

Get the picture? No matter what happens it *always* comes back to empowering *you*. Only *you* can change your core negative beliefs. Catch those thoughts as they happen. Change them into positive thoughts and you will see the beginning of a new you.

You don't have to be a victim any longer. It doesn't matter where the negative messages came from, just practice catching them in the act and befriend them. Yes, *befriend* them. That's the way to make an ally out of a former enemy. It's your responsibility if you want to change.

> *If a man repeats a lie over and over,*
> *he will eventually accept the lie as truth.*
> *Moreover he will BELIEVE it to be the truth.*
> ~ Napoleon Hill

Chapter 18

Compassionate Communication

Be kind, for everyone you meet is fighting a hard battle.
~ Plato

"That treatment plan you wrote for Jon stinks! I don't know what you were thinking!!" exclaimed the psychiatric nurse. She stood in my office at the Rehabilitation Facility, red faced and ready for a fight. I hesitated, and for the first time in my life, listened to what was in another person's heart, rather than automatically reacting to the words coming out of their mouth. Surprised at what I "heard," I genuinely responded, "Wow Jackie, you really care."

Jackie stood looking at me, dumbfounded, for a moment. Then she realized I was being sincere, and replied, "Well of course I care! And, honestly, your treatment plan isn't so bad... What I'm *really* upset about is that director of nursing. Do you have time to talk?"

That conversation happened in the fall of 2000, and it changed my life. I had just returned from my first Compassionate Communication weekend training with psychologist Dr. Marshall Rosenberg. I did what he suggested: I really listened. It had immediate and powerful results. I have been practicing what I learned ever since.

Conflict is always present in our world,
people and nations have differences,
avoiding conflict won't help, nor will violence.
Peace is attained through embracing conflict with inclusion,
understanding and compassion.
~ Albert Einstein

The Value of a Listening Ear

What I "heard" in Jackie's heart was what she was feeling and needing. She cared about her severely mentally ill clients, and was upset that she wasn't respected and appreciated by "the system." She had been working for over thirty years as a psychiatric nurse and was burned out. Overworked and underpaid; that's what her negativity was about. Her anger wasn't directed at me, personally. I suspect it came my way that morning because, as an administrator, she saw me as an example of the system that she felt was abusing her.

If I hadn't taken time to use a listening ear we would probably have gotten into an argument. I would have wanted to defend the treatment plan; tell her how hard I worked on it. And I would have probably criticized her because she hadn't contributed to it.

Instead I was able to hear the feelings and needs behind her statement. I was able to sidestep an argument and support her where she was feeling unsupported.

Later I realized this style of communication was the strategy Jackie used to engage people in conversation. Unfortunately this strategy often left her with unmet needs for her own support.

If you only have a hammer,
you tend to see every problem as a nail.
~ Abraham Maslow

How this Relates to Organizing - Example #1

"My mother nags me all the time about how disorganized I am. I'm angry with her," Carole kicked the trash aside and threw some dirty socks into a hamper.

Using Compassionate Communication, I asked, "When you say your mother nags you, do you think she has a need to contribute to your wellbeing?"

Carole immediately perked up. With sparkling eyes she turned to me and replied, "Yes! She's very well intended that way... Hmmm... I think she also has a need for my safety. She's worried this place is going to turn into a fire hazard! Thanks! I love my mom and when I look at it like that I can appreciate her rather than be upset."

Earlier in our session, I had briefly introduced Carole to the concept of Compassionate Communication. I was delighted at how quickly she caught on. She immediately recognized the deeper issues of the feelings and needs, and the strategy her mother was using.

Words of comfort, skillfully administered,
are the oldest therapy known to man.
~ Louis Nizer

How this Relates to Organizing - Example #2

"I hate that Andy always puts the mail over there. It's a hassle. It goes in *this* area of the office now." Shelley motioned toward the door. "Did you tell him that you created an Inbox and moved it over here?" I asked.

"Well, not exactly, but I figure he can see that for himself." Shelley replied. "Why not ask him if he'd be willing to put the mail here now?" I asked.

A week later I returned and Shelley said she was pleased. She'd politely asked Andy if he could put the mail in the new location. He said he'd be happy to, and apologized. He said he didn't realize that's what she wanted.

Sometimes you make assumptions, and need to state what seems obvious. And sometimes you think other people can read your mind and anticipate your needs. Learning to communicate in a clear authentic way is the solution to these situations.

> *A gentle word, a kind look, a good-natured smile*
> *can work wonders and accomplish miracles.*
> ~ William Hazlitt

How this Relates to Organizing - Example #3

Tim, a hardworking chiropractor in his mid-thirties, grumbled as he filed some papers, "My mother's overbearing."

"Sounds like your need for independence isn't being met?" I asked.

He looked surprised, and hesitated for a moment. "Well, that's exactly right! How did you know? I like to organize things my own way and she tells me all the time how they should be done. It makes me crazy."

We spoke further and did some problem solving. We talked about ways Tim could set healthy boundaries with his mother. One of them was by using a technique called Broken Record.

Broken Record

The Broken Record technique is when you kindly and firmly tell someone, "No." And when they ask again, you politely repeat "No." Each time they ask you, smile and pleasantly repeat variations on your answer of *no*. Eventually they'll understand that you're not going to change your answer.

The Broken Record technique is useful if you need to set a boundary. With regard to organizing, if you're downsizing, or simplifying your life, and someone offers to give you something you don't want, in a simple and friendly way, say, "No, but thank you." Or if someone tries to involve you in an activity and you are unable to oblige, say, "I'm sorry, I can't do that right now." And be prepared with an answer in case the person asks you, "Why not?"

This might take some practice. You may not have learned how to kindly, firmly say *no*. You may feel obligated. Or you may have been taught you *should* say yes and you *have to* say yes, even when it's detrimental to your well-being. Or you may have learned to lie, rather than just politely refuse.

Or you may initially say *no*, and then give in when they persist. If you say *no* and then don't stick with *no*, you teach the person that if they continue to ask, you'll eventually give in. This may reinforce their attempts to wear you down.

Sometimes it's helpful to explain yourself.
Usually a brief explanation will do.
~ Joyce B. Wilde

Enemy Images

When you characterize someone using a label such as a nag or judge them as overbearing you create what Dr. Rosenberg calls an enemy image. And you've been taught to perceive the enemy as attacking you and to respond by defending yourself -- and sometimes by attacking back -- often in subtle and covert ways, like by slamming a drawer, muttering under your breath, or complaining about them behind their back. This can be extremely painful behavior, especially when it's directed at people you love.

When you create enemy images, you get into "us versus them" thinking. This kind of thinking causes problems rather than solutions; it divides rather than unites. When you think this way, pretty much no matter what you say, the other person can feel the negative energy inside you.

It's not easy to change your perceptions, so if you do see someone as the enemy, take into consideration what the Dalai Lama said:

In the practice of tolerance, one's enemy is the best teacher.

A Few Communication Basics

It isn't always *what* you say but *how* you say it, *when* you say it, and your intention in saying it. Approximately 80 percent of communication is non-verbal (be careful with rolling your eyes, for example).

Timing is also important. A good way to find out if the timing is right is to preface what you're going to say with, "Is this a good time for me to talk about how we should file our warranty information?" or "Do you have a few minutes to help me organize the laundry room?"

Compassionate Communication works when it's sincerely done, not as a manipulation. People can usually feel or sense when it's about you and you're trying to get your own way rather than meet their needs. Make sure you're as interested in meeting their needs as your own.

Think win-win.
~ Stephen Covey

Ask Yourself:

- Am I willing to try a new approach to communication?
- Am I willing to listen?
- Am I willing to listen to people's feeling and needs, and the strategies they're using to meet their needs?
- Am I willing to take responsibility for my part when things don't work out?
- Am I willing to find ways to create win-win situations?

Interdependence and Communication

The world is rapidly changing and becoming more interconnected by the Internet and other media. Collaborative rather than competitive strategies are increasingly the answer to disharmony.

Over 50 million Americans are living in multi-generational situations today. This is in great contrast to the trend that began after World War II when independent living became more the norm. As a result, people are living in more interdependent situations.

Whether it's at work or at home, good relationships are one of the keys to success. And good communication is essential to creating relationships that are powerful, mutually empowering, and fun.

I'm writing a follow-up book titled, *"The Wilde Woman's Guide to Communicating in Five Simple Steps: Compassionate Communication Made Easy."* In that guide I'll share more ideas and tips on how to create and enjoy effective interpersonal dialogue using Compassionate Communication.

People are unreasonable, illogical, and self-centered.
Love them anyway.
~ Mother Teresa

Chapter 19

Mind the Gap

To the mind that is still, the whole universe surrenders.

~ Lao Tzu

Normally when you think about organizing, phrases like, "I'm going to get organized once and for all!" come to mind. Rather than trying to force things, or rush forward, why not try approaching life in a discerning way, with mindfulness?

I mentioned one definition of mindfulness in Chapter 5. Here's another: "The quality or state of being conscious or aware of something."

Mindfulness is achieved through an ongoing practice and intentionality (being deliberate or purposeful). Practicing mindfulness can help integrate these five steps in your life. Here's how:

Head/Heart Balance

Pay attention as you carry out Step One and let go, simplify, and reduce the flow in. Observe when your head makes a decision that doesn't support your heart's desire. Cultivate a head/heart balance.

There's a lot of symbolism in the amount of heart *"dis-ease"* that's prevalent in our modern day society. Allow time for the emotional experiences of shame, guilt, and grief (and other emotions) to take place; but then take the time to resolve them. This is an individual process; trust your intuition and let it guide you.

When you let go, there's typically a gap in time before something new comes into your life. Mind the gap.

What literally does *mind the gap* mean? It's a caution to train passengers in London to be careful while crossing the space between the door and the station platform.

This train analogy is fitting because when you take time to organize, it's like stopping a locomotive. You open the door, pull out the cargo and examine it. Reassess the inventory and decide if what you're traveling with is still relevant to your current lifestyle, needs and values.

Remember, limit the flow in; be careful with the merchandise you pick up. Pay attention to thoughts like, "This will make my life better" that drive compulsive shopping.

Mindfulness

Continuing with the train analogy: with Step Two you put back only the items you want to continue traveling with as you place them in categories. Then when you're finished, be mindful as you step over the space between train and platform.

The cargo has been reassessed and rearranged, and at this point you may be feeling a little disoriented. The train will restart its engines, and you'll be carrying a lighter load as the "new you" heads off in the direction you want to go.

Think of this process like a snake shedding its skin. It can be very revealing.

If you're struggling, mindfulness will allow you to relax into the moment, and to recognize when your brain has attached itself to a negative thought or story. Catch those thoughts and choose to replace them with positive ones.

Choice: That's the key. You can't always control what's "out there" (circumstances), but you can control your reaction to them. It may not seem like you have a choice, but on *some* level in *some* ways, you *always* have *some* choice in every situation. Practicing mindfulness allows you to become aware of your choices and exercise them in the most positive ways.

> *Between stimulus and response there is a space.*
> *In that space is our power to choose our response.*
> *In our response lies our growth and our freedom.*
> ~ Viktor Frankl

Meditation

As you carry out Step Three and work from general to specific it is typical to feel overwhelmed. Take a deep breath, slow down and be more fully present in the moment.

Consider spending some time each day in meditation. Sit still and focus on your breathing. And if you find you are more a human *doing* than a human *being,* and can't sit still, find a teacher, class or app to help you.

Remember when you were a kid and jumped into a lake? The water became brown because you stirred up all the silt. It took time for the sediment to settle, and the water to become clear again. This is the best analogy to illustrate the value of daily meditation. It brings clarity to your life, and to the organizing process. Because often when you begin to organize, things temporarily become worse before they become better. It takes a bit of time for things to settle back into place.

Sitting still can also be an effective way to get to the roots of any discomfort you experience. It allows the uneasiness to settle, and allows understandings and insights to bubble up to the light of day. Meditation is helpful for a variety of reasons, and it is powerful in combination with a regular yoga practice.

You must learn to be still in the midst of activity,
and to be vibrantly alive in repose.
~ Indira Gandhi

Talk it Out

Next, carry out Step Four and change your environment so that it supports the current version of you. Talking things through may be helpful at this point. Remember, this process is a lot like updating computer software, and it takes time for your psyche to absorb the changes.

If you can't find a family member or friend to talk to, there are great professional listeners: coaches, counselors, and therapists. Choose someone safe and nonjudgmental.

If you decide on a family member or friend, it may help to prepare them ahead of time. Let them know that you'll be making some changes and may need some emotional assistance--or "emergency empathy" as Dr. Rosenberg calls it. And when you call, immediately tell them that you need a listening ear and a compassionate response.

The dialogue you assign to the experiential
will determine whether you enjoy it or not.
~ William Rock, Artist

Write it Out

If you find you're sabotaging yourself as you carry out Step Five -- creating reminders and visual cues -- try writing. Use a stream of consciousness style and journal on a regular basis. Put pen to paper or fingers to keyboard and acknowledge what you're feeling and thinking. Don't shame yourself. Don't beat yourself up if you catch yourself being negative; you're just feeding the cycle. Use Compassionate Communication to change the negative thoughts to positive ones.

Write from your heart. Don't edit. Don't judge. Express everything that's in you. This is the place where you can gain insights, and make peace with your past, present and future. And, of course, make sure this is done in private and that no one else will see your writing (unless you want them to).

The ability to observe without evaluating
is the highest form of intelligence.
~ Jiddu Krishnamurti

Working Meditation

If you aren't the "meditation type" or the "talking type" or the "writing type," but like the idea of letting things settle, do some task or activity that lets you operate on autopilot for a while. Try gardening, cooking, or craft making. Be purposeful in how you use this time; deliberately encourage your mind to be quiet. The value in a "working meditation" or an "active meditation" is that you can get something done, *and* have time to sort things out and let them settle.

If you like to walk, try walking alone. It may also have the same effect. It's very different than walking with a friend and talking.

When walking, walk. When eating, eat.
~ Thich Nhat Hanh

Chapter 20

Hire a Professional

The secret of change is to focus all of your energy,
not on fighting the old, but on building the new.
~ Socrates

"I'll just get a friend or family member to help me."

My sister was watching me decide what to let go of while downsizing, and in the most well intended way, she said, "You can't get rid of those rubber stamps, I love them!" Five years later, I still have them, and haven't used them. (She gave me permission to share that with you.)

It's normal for friends and family members to bring their opinions, biases, expectations, and feelings about obligation. The fact that they may not be neutral to your belongings, thoughts, and feelings may present a challenge when enlisting help from them.

Self-referencing

"Self-referencing" is one dynamic that may come into play as you process your stuff with a friend or family member. Here's an example of how it works: if someone complains about their mother, the other person in the conversation thinks about themselves (rather than your situation); they think about *their* mother, or even how *they're* doing as a mother.

So when you decide to let go of that chipped tea cup that Aunt Leslie gave you, your sister thinks about how much she loved Aunt Leslie. And she tells you she can't bear the thought of letting go of that physical item that represents her love. Belongings may also represent the love you *wished* you'd gotten from someone -- or other emotional burden.

Life is a tragedy full of joy.
~ Bernard Malamud

"I Need a Witness!"

I was at a networking event and introduced myself as a professional organizer to a young man. He replied, "Oh, I'd love to do that! I'd tell them, 'Just throw that away!!'"

Those words are similar to "Just get over it." If it were that easy, we'd be living in a very different world. Typically, I encounter situations like this:

"I just need someone to tell my stories to before I let these things go," said Cary.

And Emma, "I need a witness! I need someone to see me and hear me and just be here for me as I decide what to keep and what to let go of."

The fact is that people are good.
Give people affection and security, and they will give
affection and be secure in their feelings and their behavior.
~ Abraham Maslow

Fear of Being Judged

"My children want to put me on the show 'Hoarders.' I'm not that bad, am I!?" Marie cried to me.

You may hesitate to engage a professional because you don't want people to know you have a whole house that is uninhabitable because it's full of stuff. Or your closets are packed so tight you can't open the doors. Or you can't have guests over because the guest bedroom is overflowing with Christmas decorations. Or your garage has so many things in it you can't get the car in. Or your attic is rapidly becoming a fire trap. It's overwhelming and you don't know where to begin.

Sound familiar?

Perhaps your scenario is a little less challenging. Your office and home look neat, but that's because you're a "concealer." You've put everything behind doors and in drawers. However, you haven't learned to be organized; and it's keeping you from reaching your potential.

One way or another, it's uncomfortable and you want to keep on the polite social mask that tells others you've got your act together. You're afraid someone would judge you harshly if they knew you were unorganized. If this is what you're thinking, please understand: you're normal.

The highest courage is to dare to appear to be what one is.
~ John Lancaster Spalding

The Right Fit

If you *do* hire a professional organizer, be discerning about the person with whom you work. Are they the right fit for you? Does their approach, energy, and method suit you? Sometimes if you're really sensitive, you can tell by their outgoing voicemail greeting if they resonate with you, or put you off. Then pay close attention to the initial conversation with them.

Ask them about their approach. Perhaps they have a background and experiences similar to yours, or ones that are complementary? Do they seem like they'd understand you?

Some organizers are very assertive in their approach; you may need that. Other organizers are gentle and very accommodating. Neither is right or wrong. It's just important that you find the right fit for you. See if you can have one trial session before committing to multiple sessions or anything big, expensive, or long-term. And make sure you hire someone you can learn from, rather than become dependent upon.

Give a man a fish and you feed him for a day.
Teach a man to fish and you feed him for a lifetime.
~ Chinese Proverb

Thinking vs. Doing

Thinking about something is different from the emotions that happen when you actually *do* it. A lot of times when people contact me, it's apparent they've hit their bottom and want to "get organized." Then when they actually try it, they're surprised at how challenging it is.

I equate it to going to yoga classes. I can do yoga for an hour or more when I go to a class, but at home the best I can manage is about 20 minutes (tops). You could also compare it to hiring a personal trainer rather than going alone to the gym.

It can also be motivating to hire a professional because you'll tend to want to prepare for them. Even though I reassure people that this isn't *necessary*, it can be a good side benefit. After all, you're spending time, money and energy. You've made a commitment to change, and are taking the actions necessary to do so. It helps to have someone who's encouraging you and holding you accountable.

Nothing is impossible, the word itself says 'I'm possible!'
~ Audrey Hepburn

Reframing

A professional can also help you "reframe" challenges into opportunities for growth and change. Think of it like this: If you have blue lenses in your glasses, and look at a lemon, you'll mistake it for a lime. It can be very hard to grasp that the object's appearance really is in the eye of the beholder.

A professional can also help you articulate your goals and stay the course until you achieve them. They can give you moral support, validation, and be a great cheerleader. You won't meet your goals if you are blocking them with negative thoughts that create nonproductive behaviors that prevent positive outcomes.

Most people never learn the art of transmuting their strongest emotions into dreams of a constructive nature.
~ Napoleon Hill

A professional should not impose their ego or try to control the situation. Rather, they serve you best when they take a collaborative problem-solving approach. Teamwork can be powerful.

Summary

Many people are struggling with too much stuff. It isn't something we advertise, so we don't realize that others are in the same boat.

Use these five steps as guidelines and create what works for you. If you're still having trouble, contact me and I'll help.

Have the courage to follow your heart and intuition.
They somehow already know what you truly want to become.
~ Steve Jobs

About the Author

Our background and circumstances may have influenced who we are,
but we are responsible for who we become.
~ Cicero, Rome (106-43 B.C.)

When I read a book, especially a how-to book, I often wonder, who is this person? What have they done in their life? Why are they qualified to write about this subject? How do *I* know *they* know what they're talking about? And how do I know they walk their talk?

Here's a quick thumbnail sketch of who I am, what I've done, and what I'm doing now. You can determine if my experiences and perspective resonate with you:

Joyce Wilde's background in restaurant ownership, mental health, and law enforcement—and her decades of recovery from alcoholism—give her unique insight into organizing and transitioning issues.

Joyce stopped drinking in 1989. The catalyst was her sister's death in a drunken driving accident. On Joyce's ninth day of sobriety, her father, a recovering alcoholic himself, died of a heart attack.

A few years later, she transitioned into a new life by selling her ownership in a restaurant/bar business and returning to school. She received a Master of Science degree in Clinical Psychology. Over the next fourteen years she worked as Senior Researcher at the UCLA - Neuropsychiatric Institute at Camarillo State Hospital; as a Residential Director of an unlocked Psychiatric Rehabilitation Facility; and as Program Administrator for a Crisis Intervention Team training program for eleven Ventura County, California, law enforcement agencies.

In each scenario, she used organizing methods which she developed and refined. Those organizing efforts in conjunction with her own recovery from compulsive drinking, smoking, eating, and shopping have given her a clear understanding of how to manage effectively the thoughts and behaviors that are the roots of disorganization.

Joyce loves to share effective ways to address core issues that lead to challenges with organizing effectively, communicating compassionately, and transitioning smoothly. She has been meditating daily for nearly a dozen years; and her understanding of mindfulness comes from this practice.

Her clientele include business people and retired professionals who express their appreciation for her authenticity and ability to deal with delicate issues in a clear and straightforward manner. Her personal challenges and work experiences equip her to identify obstacles others face and help them change their habits into positive, productive, and healthy lifestyles.

Appendix A: The Benefits of Organizing

Begin today what seemed impossible yesterday.
~ Anonymous

To leave you on an encouraging note, here are some of the benefits of organizing. You can get more focused, and have increased order, simplicity, and ease. And...

Organizing Can Save You Money by:

- Finding money, gift cards, stamps, and coupons.
- Finding items that can be reused like wrapping paper, envelopes, and boxes.
- Finding items that may be "re-gifted" in the future.
- Knowing where items are located, rather than having to replace them.
- Paying bills on time, and sending for rebates.
- Returning library items on time.
- Donating to a charity and getting a receipt for tax purposes.
    AND - you can make money by selling your items!

Organizing Can Save You Energy by:

- Experiencing less frustration -- due to a sense of control.
- Feeling happier and more satisfied with your surroundings.
- Not wasting time finding things -- especially when you're busy.
- Eliminating embarrassment when people come to visit and you need to hurry to clean and put things in order.

Organizing Can Be Fun Because of:

- Finding things to use and appreciate again (decorations, photos, jewelry, and mementos).
- The feeling of accomplishment when you have created a system of organization that allows you to find things easily.
- Keeping family members and friends abreast of your progress and benefits.
- Freeing up your energy to do new things!

The adventure you're ready for is the one you get.
~ Joseph Campbell

Appendix B: Summary of the Five Simple Steps

The great thing in this world is not so much where you stand,
as in what direction you are moving.
~ Oliver Wendell Holmes

Step One: Let go. Simplify. Reduce the Flow in

Let go of what you can. Remove what no longer makes sense. Keep what you love and need. Like computer software, update to the best current version of yourself. Whittle down to the essentials. Warning: This step puts you face-to-face with decision-making, and quite possibly, with guilt, grief, shame -- and sources of pleasure. It is frequently not until you become clear on what you *don't* want, that you are successful in creating and embracing what you *do* want. Begin to connect your heart with your head.

Step Two: Create Categories. And Use Them

Establish and use categories by asking yourself questions like: *"Where will I look for this next time?"* and *"Where will I look for this, first, when I need it again?"* If you're not sure, ask yourself, *"What is the broad category in which this item belongs?"* (Work or home? Which room?) Carry out this same process on your computer. Create accurately named folders and documents. Use what comes to mind first, without second guessing your answer. To stay organized, *use* the categories you create. Begin to connect your head with your hands.

Step Three: Work from General to Specific

Organize by working from general to specific. Keep an eye on the big picture, and don't get too precise until needed. This will keep you from getting overwhelmed, as it can feel like you're trying to "wrap your arms around an elephant." Keep things as simple and straightforward as possible. When you become aware that you're getting hyper-focused or distracted, "notice and adjust." For example, if an office needs to be organized, don't focus for two hours on one drawer, keep the whole office in your focus.

Step Four: Keep Closest What You Use Most Often

And keep closest what makes life convenient, what's useful, beautiful, feels good, or makes sense. Position the items around you in a way that makes them most user-friendly based on your day-to-day living. In your office, this means keeping your Hot Projects closest, positioning your Warm Projects further away, and putting your Cold Projects out of the way. Let go of your Dead Projects, or put them into archives. Pay attention to how the items around you make you *feel*, as well as what you *think* of them. Bring more awareness to how you move through time and space.

Step Five: Create and Use Visual Cues

Create visual cues to remind yourself what to do, and when to do it. Use one calendar. Record things as soon as possible, and update them. Visual cues may be sophisticated in electronic form, or as simple as a well placed sticky note. Don't try to hold too many details in your head. That can create stress. There are too many distractions in the world today. Experiment. *Learn* what works for you, and *do* what works for you. Don't worry about how others organize themselves. There's no right way, there's only what supports you best.

Organizing is a Process

Remember, organizing is not an *event*. It is a *process,* and, like a garden, things need to be weeded and sorted on a regular basis. Learn to implement these five steps *as a lifestyle* and you will be able to focus on the activities you love -- and stay organized at the same time.

> *Order and simplification are the first steps*
> *toward the mastery of a subject.*
> ~ Thomas Mann

- -

✂   Cut here to take this with you as a handy reference   ✂

Summary of the Five Simple Steps

Step One: Let go. Simplify. Reduce the Flow in

Step Two: Create Categories. And Use Them

Step Three: Work from General to Specific

Step Four: Keep Closest What You Use Most Often

Step Five: Create and Use Visual Cues

Appendix C: Books

There are many gates to the house of wisdom.

~ Edward Counsel

Adams, Keith, *Pearls of Wisdom: Quotations to Stimulate Your Mind, Heart, and Soul* (CreateSpace Independent Publishing Platform, 2013).

Allen, David, *Getting Things Done: The Art of Stress-Free Productivity* (Penguin Books, 2001).

Anonymous, *Alcoholics Anonymous* (New York: Alcoholics Anonymous Publishing, Inc., 1955).

Anonymous, *The Key: And the Name of the Key is Willingness* (Mountain View, California: A Center for the Practice of Zen Buddhist Meditation, 1984).

Bacci, Ingrid, *The Art of Effortless Living* (Bantam, 2002).

Bridges, William, *Transitions: Making Sense of Life's Changes* (Perseus Books Group, 2004).

Cagan, Andrea, *Peace Is Possible: The Life and Message of Prem Rawat* (Mighty River Press, 2006).

Cameron, Julia, *The Artist's Way: A Spiritual Path to Higher Creativity* (Penguin Group, 1992).

Cameron, Julia, *The Artist's Way Every Day: A Year of Creative Living* (Tarcher, 2009).

Carnegie, Dale, *How to Win Friends and Influence People* (Simon & Shuster Inc., 1936).

Carr, Allen, *Allen Carr's Easy Way for Women to Stop Smoking* (Arcturus Publishing Limited, 2005).

Carson, Richard, D., *Taming Your Gremlin: A Guide to Enjoying Yourself* (Harper & Row, Publishers, Inc., 1983).

Caye, Hana Haatainen, *Green Grandma's Vinegar Fridays* (Self Published, 2011. Found on Amazon.com).

Chödrön, Pema, *Start Where You Are: A Guide to Compassionate Living* (Shambhala, 2001).

Chödrön, Pema, *When Things Fall Apart: Heart Advice for Difficult Times* (Shambhala, 2000).

Covey, Stephen, R., *The 7 Habits of Highly Effective People: Powerful Lessons in Personal Change* (DC Books, 2005).

Earll, Bob, *I Got Tired of Pretending: How an Adult Raised in An Alcoholic/Dysfunctional Family Finds Freedom* (STEM Publications, 1988).

Eden, Donna, and Feinstein, David, *Energy Medicine: Balancing Your Body's Energies for Optimal Health, Joy, and Vitality* (Penguin Group, 2008).

Feldman, Dara, *The Heart of Education: Bringing Joy, Meaning and Purpose Back to Teaching and Learning* (Motivational Press, Inc., 2013).

Hanh, Thich Nhat, *The Art of Power* (HarperOne, 2008).

Hawkins, David R., *Power vs. Force: The Hidden Determinants of Human Behavior* (Hay House, 2002).

Hill, Napoleon, *Think and Grow Rich* (Napoleon Hill Foundation, 2012).

Jeffers, Susan, *Feel the Fear and Do it Anyway* (Ballantine Books, 1998).

Johnson, Spencer, *Who Moved My Cheese?* (Penguin Putnam, Inc., 1998).

Maull, Fleet, *Dharma in Hell: The Prison Writings of Fleet Maull* (Prison Dharma Network, 2005).

Myers, Wayland, *Nonviolent Communication: The Basics As I Know and Use Them* (Wayland Myers, 1998).

Pendyala, Krishna, and Vargo, Mike, *Beyond the PIG and the APE: Realizing SUCCESS and true HAPPINESS* (Big YOU Media, 2011).

Pick, Marcelle, *Amazing Wellness Magazine: Are You Tired or Wired?* (Active Interest Media, 2013).

Rosenberg, Marshall B., *Nonviolent Communication: A Language of Life* (Puddledancer Press, 2003).

Rosenberg, Marshall B., *Nonviolent Communication Companion Workbook: A Practical Guide for Individual, Group or Classroom Study* (Puddledancer Press, 2003).

Tolle, Eckhart, *The Power of Now: A Guide to Spiritual Enlightenment* (New World Library, 2004).

Tolle, Eckhart, *A New Earth: Awakening to Your Life's Purpose* (Penguin, 2008).

Welchons, John E., *Awakening from Grief: Finding the Way Back to Joy* (New World Library, 2003).

Wilson, James, *Adrenal Fatigue: The 21st Century Stress Syndrome* (Smart Publications, 2001).

Appendix D: Websites

It's not what you look at that matters, it's what you see.
~ Henry David Thoreau

www.bdpromarketing.com

Your resource for creative marketing. BD-PRo Marketing Solutions provides tools and resources to help you grow your business through innovative marketing techniques.

www.cnvc.org

Center for Nonviolent Communication: An International Organization. Based on the work of Dr. Marshall B. Rosenberg, and the principles of nonviolence -- the natural state of compassion when no violence is present in the heart.

www.cvetan.com

Mary Cvetan is a multi-talented freelance writer who provides a variety of services including for B2B and B2C copywriting for print and digital media.

www.fleetmaull.com

Fleet Maull is an author, master teacher/trainer and servant leader who facilitates deep transformation for individuals and organizations through his *Radical Responsibility* philosophy and trainings.

www.greengrandma.org

A blog focused on common sense healthier and greener living, with a dose of grandmotherly advice mixed in.

www.johndedakis.com

John DeDakis is an author, manuscript editor and writing workshop leader.

www.krishnapendyala.com

A site to learn about innate human drives that evolved to feed and protect us. A lack of awareness of these drives can easily sabotage our chances for true happiness and success.

www.lindakallus.com

I am an Energy Medicine Practitioner and Artist. I coach people in Emotional Freedom Technique (EFT/Tapping), and self-care Energy Medicine. As an artist I work in various mediums.

www.mindfulchoices.org

A blog to explore the tricks our mind can play and how our hidden inner drives influence our choice-making.

www.networkprotoolkit.com

This website contains a powerful online toolkit that will help you turn your networking into profits. Learn how to expand your professional network, uncover more qualified business opportunities and boost your confidence and success.

www.suzanneferguson.com

Spiritual Mastery Coaching helps you navigate the path to your true self.

www.wopg.org

Words of Peace Global is an international charitable foundation comprised of volunteers, supported by a small staff team, who share this perspective on peace, and are inspired by the work of Prem Rawat.

www.wordsinyourmouth.com

Speechless is a copywriting, editing, and voice-over business offering personalized service to clients worldwide.

6150858R00088

Made in the USA
San Bernardino, CA
02 December 2013